I DARE *YOU* TO CHANGE!

FOREWORD BY CRAIG GROESCHEL
Pastor, LifeChurch.tv

I DARE *YOU* TO CHANGE!

Discover the Difference Between Dreaming of a Better Life and Living It

Bil Cornelius

New York, New York

I Dare You to Change!

ISBN-13: 978-0-8249-4818-4

Published by Guideposts
16 East 34th Street
New York, New York 10016
www.guideposts.com

Distributed by Ideals Publications, a division of Guideposts
2636 Elm Hill Pike, Suite 120
Nashville, TN 37214

Guideposts and *Ideals* are registered trademarks of Guideposts.

Acknowledgments

Every attempt has been made to credit the sources of copyrighted material used in this book. If any such acknowledgment has been inadvertently omitted or miscredited, receipt of such information would be appreciated.

All Scripture quotations, unless otherwise noted, are taken from *The Holy Bible, New International Version*. Copyright © 1973, 1978, 1984 International Bible Society. Used by permission of Zondervan Bible Publishers.

Scripture quotations marked (KJV) are taken from *The King James Version of the Bible*.

Scripture quotations marked (NAS) are taken from the *New American Standard Bible*, copyright © 1960, 1962, 1963, 1968, 1971, 1972, 1973, 1975, 1977, 1995 by the Lockman Foundation. Used by permission.

Scripture quotations marked (NCV) are taken from *The Holy Bible, New Century Version*. Copyright © 2005 by Thomas Nelson, Inc. Used by permission. All rights reserved.

Scripture quotations marked (NLT) are taken from the *Holy Bible*, New Living Translation. Copyright © 1996. Used by permission of Tyndale House Publishers, Inc., Wheaton, Illinois 60189. All rights reserved.

Scripture quotations marked (NRSV) are taken from the *New Revised Standard Version Bible*. Copyright © 1989 by the Division of Christian Education of the National Council of the Churches of Christ in the U.S.A. Used by permission. All rights reserved.

Library of Congress Cataloging-in-Publication Data

Cornelius, Bil, 1972-
   I dare you to change! : discover the difference between dreaming of a new life and living it / Bil Cornelius.
    p. cm.
 ISBN 978-0-8249-4818-4
 1. Change (Psychology)–Religious aspects–Christianity. 2. Dreams–Religious aspects–Christianity. 3. Success–Religious aspects–Christianity. 4. Self-actualization (Psychology)–Religious aspects–Christianity. I. Title.
 BV4599.5.C44C67 2010
 248.4–dc22

                                                              2010017000

Cover design by James Iacobelli and Georgia Morrissey
Cover photograph by Monica Carrion
Interior design by Gretchen Schuler-Dandridge
Typeset by Aptara

Printed and bound in the United States of America
10 9 8 7 6 5 4 3 2 1

CONTENTS

FOREWORD

"This is just the way I am," I confidently told my counselor.

At the tender age of twenty-six, I was a candidate to become an ordained minister. Several church leaders who were overseeing my journey toward ordination were convinced I was a workaholic and needed help to change. I was convinced they were wrong. *They just don't know how much I care about God and His church*, I rationalized.

This wise and caring panel of ministers asked me to take a week off to contemplate my priorities and consider what changes I could make that would give me the endurance to go the distance. Knowing this was a battle I couldn't win, I agreed, although, honestly, I never planned to slow my frenzied pace.

When they later discovered that I didn't take the week off but instead continued working feverishly, they assigned me to mandatory counseling to address my workaholic tendencies. I found myself sitting quietly in a little chair, facing a well-intentioned counselor. He reviewed his notes, mumbled a little to himself, looked up at me, and said, "You really don't think you can change, huh?" Convinced this was just the way I was, I explained how I couldn't lessen my drive to work.

I'll never forget what happened next. He leaned in and lovingly, not much above a whisper, said, "So what you're telling me is, even our God isn't big enough to help you change."

He got me.

Maybe you can relate. *This is just the way I am. I'm always going to be like this. Nothing is ever going to change for me.* If you've ever felt like you're in a rut, you're not alone. But God has directed you to the perfect book: *I Dare You to Change!* by Bil Cornelius is a spiritually charged, inspiring, and very practical book that will empower you to walk toward the life you've always hoped for.

Maybe you feel like you're stuck in a dead-end job or you'll never have a happy marriage. Bil will show you that you are not who you *think* you are, but who *God* says you are! You can change. You can do all things through Christ who gives you strength. You can live a life that matters.

Turn the page, buckle your seat belt, and let the journey begin.

—Craig Groeschel
Pastor, LifeChurch.tv

I DARE *YOU* TO CHANGE!

INTRODUCTION

I once counseled a young couple who were newlyweds and really committed to each other and to the Lord. The husband—I'll call him Dave—was working hard to get ahead in his job, but every time we met, he spoke to me about his dream of starting his own business. Every time we met, I heard the same story: "I feel like there's more I could be doing. I want to get into real estate, build a business."

I could tell Dave needed a push, so one day I said to him, "Dave, you're talking it, you're dreaming it, but you're not doing anything about it. You and I are not going to meet again until you've done something to start making this dream a reality. Don't make another appointment with me until you've purchased your first rental property."

At first Dave was shocked that I'd say such a thing. But within six months, he had bought not one but two rental properties. Now he's well on his way to building a nice real-estate portfolio and has even started another business on the side with income about to surpass that of his regular job. Dave is not unusual. He started out with the same desire for a better life that most people have, but he didn't know how to get started and achieve what he wanted. He had to find out that it's not just a matter of hoping; it's about stepping out and becoming

1

comfortable with the risk involved. It's about going from dreaming of a better life to putting down goals and giving them a deadline.

For as long as I've been working with people, the basic questions they ask never seem to change:

"How can I make my life better for myself and my family?"
"Why do I face so many challenges?"
"Why do I never seem to get ahead?"
"How do I get my act together?"
"How can I make my life meaningful?"
"Does everyone else have trouble feeling fulfilled?"
"Why does it seem I always have to settle for less?"

Maybe you're asking these questions too. Don't you wish you could find some practical answers?

I've spent my adult life helping people respond to the challenges we all face. I'm constantly confronted by the stress, burnout, poor health, lack of direction, inefficiency, indecision, and stagnation that plague Americans today. But things like this don't discourage me because I know we can find our way out of these problems. I know that because *I* changed.

> "To take the leaps?
> A provocative question
> is the only way that
> I've found."
> — JAMES F. BANDROWSKI

Years ago, when I was pastoring a small church in Irving, Texas, I was restless. I kept feeling that I wasn't supposed to stay there, but I wasn't sure what God wanted me to do. It was a good church, but the prospects for reaching people were limited. At times, I even began to wonder if I was going to sell used cars for the rest of my life.

I was attending seminary at the time, and there was one particular tree I would sit under, pondering my future and asking God what I was supposed to do. As I sat there one day, the idea came to me that I could start a new church. I believe God's dreams for us are so much bigger than we usually imagine. So I envisioned a place where people could be encouraged to dream big rather than stay limited. I thought about it for a while and then started putting my dream on paper. I dreamed of a place where I could bring my unchurched friends. I had a lot of high school and college buddies who wouldn't be caught dead in church. Even though church had changed my life, it wasn't working for them. It wasn't speaking their language. I knew I'd have to start something from scratch because I didn't want to try and change an existing church.

Twelve years later, I'm the pastor of Bay Area Fellowship in Corpus Christi, Texas, a church of thousands of people, most of whom had never attended a church. One of the ways we knew we'd hit our target, that we'd reached groups the church had completely neglected, was when crack pipes and drug paraphernalia, along with knives and condom wrappers, started showing up in the offering basket as tokens of a commitment to change. People who weren't comfortable with Christianity or religion as they had known it were starting to make room for God in their lives. They were being inspired to change. As I think back to those moments sitting under that tree, talking with God about His plans for my future, I'm so glad He gave me the courage to step out and realize His dreams for me.

Are you frustrated, feeling like life has more to offer than you're currently experiencing? Could it be that you have settled for less than God's best in your life? The fact that you've picked up this book says that you're looking for a change. You desire more in life, and that's a *good* thing. You have that divine discontent, and you're ready to make some important changes.

▄▄ Why Do We Fail to Experience God's Best?

I firmly believe that most people *want* to do better, get better, and live better. We don't want to settle for less; we just *don't know how* to achieve more.

We make New Year's resolutions. We read books, attend seminars, and listen to self-help podcasts. We spend time dreaming about how things could be. We keep to-do lists. We make commitments and remain hopeful for the future.

The problem is that we don't really know *how* to accomplish these things. We don't know how to reach and sustain a high level of success, happiness, and health.

We don't know how to experience God's best.

Why is that?

There are many answers to this question, of course. However, the main answer is simple, and I'll spend the rest of this book unpacking it: *Most of us don't understand that success is a process of day-to-day accomplishment.*

Success involves putting one foot in front of the other every day, concentrating on reaching small goals that will eventually add up to help you reach your biggest goals. Why don't we understand this?

Maybe it's because we live in a day of instant gratification. The world is literally at our fingertips. With the click of a computer mouse, we can order dinner, plan a vacation, run a business, or gamble our lives away. We don't just have fast-food restaurants; we have entire companies devoted to bringing dinner directly to our door. Hundreds of TV channels are available to us at the touch of a button, not to mention thousands of movies that we can watch instantly.

> Success is a process of day-to-day accomplishment.

We've been sold a bill of goods. We've been led to believe that we can gain knowledge without studying, achieve fitness by taking a pill, and raise well-adjusted children without prudent parenting. We believe we can experience real life by popping in a DVD, develop top-flight organizations through well-articulated mission statements, and build successful businesses with slick advertising campaigns.

This reminds me of a story about a forty-year-old woman who gets hit by a bus, is rushed to the hospital, and dies on the operating table. She meets God and He tells her, "Don't worry, you're not going to die right now. I still have a purpose for you, and I'm giving you forty more years." Next thing you know, she wakes up in the recovery room, thrilled to be alive. Later she thinks, "If I have forty more years, I want to make sure I look GREAT." So after she's healed from the bus accident, she immediately talks to a plastic surgeon and signs up for all kinds

> Real change is an inside job.

of work—a nip here, a tuck there. Soon, she's reworked from head to toe. After the surgery, she continues her makeover with a dark tan, a new hairstyle, and a whole new wardrobe. Her makeover complete, she's walking across the street and—*bam!*—she gets hit by a bus again, but this time she really dies. Now she's standing before God, angry, and she says, "God, what happened? You told me I had forty more years!" And God looks at her and says, "I'm sorry . . . I didn't recognize you."

It's so easy for us to think we're changing our lives when we change things on the *outside*. We believe we can get results without putting forth effort, and without the basic ingredients of perseverance, fortitude, and courage. We think that a new job, a new city, a new haircut will make everything better. *But real change is an inside job.* It starts with our attitude, our efforts, and our energy. It takes *intention* and *action* on a daily basis.

But we're not a society that understands this. It's not that people don't have talents and innate abilities; they do. Our problem is that we have lost sight of the basic hands-on how-tos of high achievement. We've forgotten that it takes *actual work* every single day to attain our goals and live the life we dream of. The key to any kind of success is day-to-day accomplishment.

Everyone has inconsistencies. We all have chasms between our ability and our actual performance. This gap keeps us from a life of achievement and makes us struggle with failure much of the time.

We take our gifts for granted, rather than intentionally developing them each and every day. We might have talents, skills, and intelligence, but we are not actively involved in the process that leads to achievement. We could perform at a high level every day, but we don't. We choose to settle for less, rather than more.

■ Solutions

For decades Sears, Roebuck and Company was a leader in retail and catalog sales. The Sears catalog was so popular that it became an icon in American culture and history. But in the 1990s, when people began shopping on the Internet, Sears was reluctant to let go of this time-tested approach and enter the world of online marketing. Why mess with success? The problem was, nobody was buying from catalogs anymore. Because of its slowness to adapt and respond to challenges in the new retail environment, Sears lost considerable market share. To this day Sears has not been able to regain the ground it lost. How simple it would have been for Sears to be on the cutting edge of technology and transfer its entire catalog to the Internet way back when we all first started shopping online.

While some people and organizations respond to challenges and grow beyond them, most utterly fail. They're still alive, but they are just getting by.

They fall short of God's blessing time after time, yet they were created to be alive, changing, and not settling for less than God's best!

Based on my experience working with people from all backgrounds, I believe anyone can break past barriers and become successful. Fulfillment is not the exclusive domain of a gifted few but a process of self-development that everyone can use to bring forth the best from themselves and others. It's a matter of managing every area of life on a daily basis. Success, as they say, is hard by the yard—but a cinch by the inch!

■ I Dare You to Change

It's time for you to begin living the life that God has always had for you. It's time to achieve your full potential.

But what is your definition of success? I'm not going to define it for you because it's different for every person. What are the areas in your life where you have been settling for less than you know God has for you?

I know a woman who is always busy. She's working two jobs, raising a family, and trying to be an active member of her church. But over the last few years she has felt a growing desire to serve her community. Her heart burns to do charity work, to work at the homeless shelter, to take part in overseas mission trips. Yet she can't seem to figure out how she will ever get from "here" to "there."

> There are two lives that we have right now. The first is the life we live. The second is the life that we *really* desire to live.

I know a man who has been a building contractor for two decades and hates it. He really wants to be a firefighter but he's paralyzed by inertia and hopelessness. How can a man of forty change careers when he has a family to support, and especially when the career he wants is usually reserved for people twenty years younger? His goal seems unreachable, so he continues in his same job, always wishing he were somewhere else.

Are you like these people? Tired of being less, doing less, having less?

Today you can make a decision. By the end of this introduction, I pray that you will make an important choice, a life choice. My prayer is that you will choose to never settle for anything less than God's best for you in every area of your life. But my prayer is that God will motivate you and fire you up! It's not me who's daring you to change. It's God.

God *does* have a better life for you, a better life than you ever dreamed possible. We all live two lives. The first is the life we live. The second is the life that we really desire to live. We want to have that life, but most of the time we live a completely different life than the one we dream about. That second life is within us, dying to get out.

In the movie *Falling Down*, Michael Douglas plays a character named William who has reached the end of his rope. He's completely frustrated with life and people and the hopelessness of it all. If you've seen this movie, you might remember the scene where William enters a fast-food restaurant and begins to order breakfast. "I'm sorry, we've stopped serving breakfast," the cashier tells him.

> "Decide that you want it more than you are afraid of it."
>
> — BILL COSBY

"But I want breakfast," William says.

William talks to the manager but grows more frustrated. All the time he keeps repeating, "I just want some breakfast."

Finally he pulls an automatic weapon out of his bag. All the customers scream and panic. William tells everyone to calm down, because he *just wants some breakfast.*

William has reached the end of his rope, the point where the status quo just won't do anymore. He is now willing to do anything to change his reality.

Maybe for you the phrase is "I just want to be happy" or "I just want a better job" or "I just want to be able to pay all my bills this month." Are you fed up with where you are? Do you have the passion and the drive to make a change? You obviously don't need to scare others like William in the fast-food restaurant, but you do need to do something unexpected, bold, and, at times, risky.

Let's go on a journey together. Let's learn to take courage and seek God's best for our lives. Let's discover how we can live that *second* life, the "unlived" life that we so desire to bring into reality. In the rest of this book we will explore the biblical story of Gideon, a man who starts out in a place where many of us are today—living in fear—but ends up leading a nation out of slavery and into freedom. As we walk with Gideon, we'll learn ten principles—ten *steps*—that will help us dare to change, find God's best, and begin living it.

How to Read This Book

I Dare You to Change! is a hands-on, how-to action plan for life. While it is possible to simply read through this book and glean principles for successful living, you will gain the most benefit if you actively put the principles into practice. Use this book to stop, think, and evaluate your own life, where you are and where you want to go.

With that in mind, I've included a section at the end of each chapter titled "Looking Back, Looking Forward," a quick recap of key principles covered thus far and some practical exercises to help you start experiencing change right away. At the very end of this section you'll find an "action plan" with a list of questions that will help you put this book's key principles into practice.

I suggest that you write your answers in a notebook and that you take the time necessary to work through every exercise carefully. If you do this, I believe you will—piece by piece, step by step—find the courage you need and make great strides in experiencing God's best for your life.

Making use of these exercises is more than a suggestion. On behalf of a God who is a God of action, I'm daring you. I'm daring you to get to work right now and start on your plan. Take these God-given principles and apply them to your life. Find the strength to change and to understand that there's a difference between dreaming of a better life and living it.

AGAIN the Israelites did evil in the eyes of the LORD, and for seven years he gave them into the hands of the Midianites.

(JUDGES 6:1)

STEP ONE

BREAK THE CYCLE OF FAILURE

Before we can experience God's best, we must break the cycle of failure.

How many times have we had this happen to us? We resolve to get out of debt, but instead we let our credit-card balance get out of control—again. We say we want to improve our marriage, but then have a fight with our spouse—again. We decide to be better parents, but then our kids disobey us and we lose our temper—again. We plan to be more responsible with our money, but overspend—again.

It seems like the problems we deal with, we deal with over and over. We're caught in a trap, a cycle of failure. Instead of going somewhere, we walk a treadmill—and our lives won't change until we get off it.

That's exactly where the nation of Israel was when Gideon came on the scene. The Old Testament book of Judges describes it this way:

> Again the Israelites did evil in the eyes of the LORD, and for seven years he gave them into the hands of the Midianites. Because the power of Midian was so oppressive, the Israelites prepared shelters for themselves in mountain clefts, caves and strongholds. (Judges 6:1–2)

The first thing that I want you to notice is the word *again*. The writer makes it clear that the Israelites were stuck in a cycle of failure.

They would sin and then God would allow their enemies to overrun them; then they would cry out to God, and finally He would deliver them. They would enjoy peace for a while, but soon the cycle would begin again. This same sequence is repeated over and over throughout the book of Judges.

What a tragedy. At this point in their history, the Israelites were living in the "land of promise," the place God had given to Abraham. This was the land "flowing with milk and honey" that Moses led them to, and that Joshua conquered. Yet as we read Judges 6, we find the children of Israel living in clefts and caves. They are scrounging around in holes in the sides of mountains, filled with fear and pain, hiding out from the Midianites.

> Pain is possibly the best motivator you can have in life.

Why had the good life in the Promised Land turned sour?

The children of Israel had disobeyed God—again. They had turned away from Him—again. And God disciplined them by handing them over—again—to captors. The Midianites and warring eastern tribes, regional bullies all, relished the role they had been given, and they gleefully taught Israel painful and costly lessons.

The truth is that we learn more from pain than we could ever learn from the good things in our lives. In his book *The Problem of Pain*, C. S. Lewis tells us, "God whispers to us in our pleasures, speaks in our conscience, but shouts in our pains; it is His megaphone to rouse a deaf world."

We hear God most clearly when pain is involved. My priorities might be out of whack, but if I get cancer, everything suddenly becomes crystal clear. Pain has an amazing way of helping us focus on what is really important.

What I am trying to say is this: Pain is your greatest advantage. The pain that you're struggling with right now can help you. It can be an incredible mentor. Pain can teach you resolve. In fact, I believe pain is possibly the best motivator you can have in life. Pain is a better motivator than pleasure will ever be. It is a better advisor than any inspirational speaker you will ever hear. Pain will bring change into your life faster than anything else you'll ever deal with.

> "If nothing changes—
> nothing changes."
> — JIM WESTLEY

The children of Israel were caught in a painful cycle. But that very pain brought about the opportunity for change.

The Threshold of Pain

Don't run away from pain. Instead, fully and deliberately experience the results of the pain you are going through. Yes, you read that last sentence correctly! It may be surprising to you that I'm telling you to embrace pain. My goal is to give you *more* pain by telling you to fully experience the effects of the pain that already exists.

No, I don't have the "spiritual gift of agitation." But I would like to agitate you, to frustrate you, or better yet, *jolt* you into taking action so you don't have to experience the same pain again.

Let me emphasize again: I want you to feel the pain. Let pain be your wake-up call—and then begin to change your life by recognizing and breaking your cycle of failure. For example, maybe your financial problems started out by celebrating each bonus or raise with a shopping spree. Or maybe your drinking first started by having a couple of cocktails or glasses of wine at the end of every day. Perhaps your weight problem began when life got busy and fast food became your regular meal. At this point, you're still able to turn things around on your own or excuse the pain away. You're still in control. But the next thing you know, creditors are calling, you're hiding your drinking from your spouse, or you've just failed another diet and are eating even more than before. At this point, you have lost control of the thing that is causing your pain. Worse, it now has control over you.

Pain is your greatest advantage.

Think back to when you were a child. Do you remember playing on a seesaw? I once heard motivational speaker Anthony Robbins say that the way pain enters our lives is often like a seesaw. Things seem to be going well, and then we suddenly experience a little pain. This little pain is like someone who is lighter than we are sitting on the other end of the seesaw. We see them and feel their weight, but because we weigh more, we aren't worried about them getting off the seesaw and letting us drop. In other words, we recognize that we aren't balanced or having fun, but we're still in control.

When we have a little pain in our lives, we often think, "I can handle it. It's fine. I'll just teeter and totter, go back and forth a bit, trying to decide whether or not I want to make a change."

We become adept at lying to ourselves.

"It's no big deal."

"I'm just a little bit overweight."

"The credit card debt isn't *that* scary."

"It's okay that this job doesn't suit me or use my natural gifting."

By refusing to change our actions, we continue to add to our pain. Worse, we often add more wrong actions and complicate our problems. And once *big* pain begins to weigh in, we lose control.

Big pain is like having someone larger than we are sitting on the other end of the seesaw. We're no longer in control of the situation. Our poor decisions have formed a bad habit that's now reaping a harvest of consequences that we *know* we don't want.

And that's a good place to be.

As soon as we realize that we no longer have control, we're ready for change. When it was just a little weight problem, it wasn't a big deal. But when the doctor tells you to prepare for diabetes and heart disease, his words help you decide to alter your lifestyle.

Likewise, it may not be a big deal to have just a little debt or just a little tight time financially. It is easy to say, "I'll keep spending what I want, when I want. It's my money. I earned it." But when the creditors call and you have no way of paying it all back, then you're ready to modify your spending habits.

> "Lord, make me so uncomfortable that I will do the very thing I fear."
>
> — RUBY DEE

Reaching the threshold of pain will lead you to a decision. It will make you cry out, "Enough! I'm ready to do whatever it takes to break this cycle." Unfortunately, most of us seem to have a very high pain threshold. We ignore pain—or worse, we are numb to it.

Just how bad did it get for the people of Israel before they reached their threshold of pain? Take a look at the following verses:

> Whenever the Israelites planted their crops, the Midianites, Amalekites and other eastern peoples invaded the country. They camped on the land and ruined the crops all the way to Gaza and did not spare a living thing for Israel, neither sheep nor cattle nor donkeys. They came up with their livestock and their tents like swarms of locusts. It was impossible to count the men and their camels; they invaded the land to ravage it. Midian so impoverished the Israelites that they cried out to the LORD for help. (Judges 6:3–6)

When you fail to handle one problem, it multiplies. Soon you have two, then three, then four, maybe five, maybe ten problems. In this case, the Midianites would get together with other nations and attack the Israelites. The Midianites, the Amalekites, and a bunch of other "-ites" were controlling the people and all of their crops. Israel's foes stole everything.

The Bible mentions that these enemies looked like a swarm of locusts throughout the land. Midianites were everywhere—attacking, swarming, and brutalizing everything. It was savage. They simply came in and overran the country, every town and every village. They came in and raped and pillaged and took everything they could grab.

They left the Israelites hopeless. Have you ever felt hopeless? Hopeless about your job? Hopeless about your marital situation or lack thereof? Hopeless about your finances? Hopeless about your kids? Hopeless about your weight or health? Hopeless about your busy schedule and stress level?

You've probably had to adjust to a bad situation here and there, but eventually one comes along that gets so bad that you finally reach your threshold, the place where your pain gets big enough that you're willing to make a change—to finally do something.

The Midianites were gaining wealth by preying on the Israelites. They were functioning as a savage nation while the Israelites were dysfunctional and ravaged. The Midianites stole their crops, cattle, donkeys, and sheep. The Israelites were losing everything fast, including their will to fight. The people who lived in the Promised Land were quickly learning to settle for way less than God's best.

The rich were getting richer, and the poor were getting poorer. That's what happens when your life is out of control. Things were going from bad to worse.

You know you're looking for the wrong solution when you don't have good crops, you don't have enough income to keep up with your needs, and you also realize that your assets are being slaughtered and diminished. The Midianites impoverished Israel. Taking their assets gave the Midianites the ability to earn an income for nothing from what the children of Israel were trying to produce.

When we don't have enough streaming income, we end up taking from our assets to pay for our liabilities. At least until the recent economic crash, people in America had been running up record amounts of credit-card debt because they continued to acquire too many liabilities, tapping into their assets (through home mortgages and home-equity loans) to pay for their gas bills, their shopping sprees, and their lavish vacations.

Do you see the problem? We wake up one day impoverished and wonder why. We let the very things that create wealth and income get eaten up and devastated. Those assets should be the last things that we consume. Yet it happens all the time. The question is whether we ignore the lessons from the experience or decide to directly face the difficulties of our circumstances.

The Israelites should have stopped and said, "Okay. You've taken our crops, but you're not going to take anything else." But they didn't. They let the Midianites steal the seed that gave them crops. Not only did the Israelites lose their income, but they also lost their ability to produce income. When they reached that point, they'd had enough.

> Pain can be your friend. Pain can help you get serious about change. I've found that pain is the greatest source of fuel to inspire lasting change.

It was impossible to count the enemies and their camels. Midian had so impoverished the Israelites that they finally cried out to the Lord for help. Israel had reached its threshold of pain. The people couldn't take it anymore. They said, "That's it, God! We're ready to turn back to you!"

When you are truly out of control, you reach what we call a "threshold of pain." This threshold is very important, because when we hit it, we finally get serious about change. It gives us the resolve to say, "That's it. This has put me out of control on the seesaw." Now the pain is heavy enough that we are no longer just talking about change. We are ready to do something about it.

Moving Beyond the Threshold of Pain

Sometimes creating change in your life means making the deep decision that will move you beyond your threshold of pain.

Maybe your pain is financial; maybe it's physical. Whatever it is, pain can be a powerful motivator.

I'd always had this dream of getting in shape, of feeling good about myself. But a funny thing happened along the way. That dream didn't motivate me to work out. It didn't motivate me to eat right, and it didn't motivate me to run.

Do you know what motivated me to do all the things that I needed to do to be in shape? It was pain. One day I glanced at a photo of myself standing beside my wife and another couple. I couldn't believe how big I looked! I tried to deny it: "It's just a bad angle," I said. Then I realized that "bad angle" was showing up in *any* picture of me. I had put on so much weight.

Maybe that is okay for some—and I don't want to compare myself with anyone else—but I just didn't like the "me" that I had become. The pain of seeing myself so overweight—and knowing that I always felt tired and out of shape—finally brought me to my own threshold of pain. I became convinced that it was time to get serious, time to finally take better care of my health.

> The threshold of pain causes us to become serious about change.

I didn't want anyone to see that picture, but I realized that wherever I went, *everybody* saw it. *I* was there, and that's what I really looked like. But rather than ignoring the issue, I decided to focus on it, acknowledge it, and commit to change.

I'm not trying to hurt you; I'm trying to help you. That's what going for God's best is all about. That is what the story of Gideon teaches us. God wants us to see a prophet who faced his fears, told the truth, and did something about the situation.

I care enough to challenge you, to plead with you to look at the painful truth. What are your greatest struggles? What is your cycle of failure? Whatever you are facing, I plead with you: *Don't do this to yourself for five more years.*

Acknowledge the pain you are facing. Experience it. Then do whatever God directs you to do to change.

The sad truth is that some of us won't be around in five years if we don't make some lifestyle changes. If we don't make some big changes in our relationships, five years from now some of us will no longer be married. If we don't make some big changes at work, five years from now some of us will be unemployed or unemployable.

> "Clear your mind of can't."
>
> — SAMUEL JOHNSON

We must look into the future—the future pain that we will experience if we do nothing to change—and face it today. In Dr. Henry Cloud's book *Nine Things You Simply Must Do*, he talks of playing a future movie of your life, thinking through the possibilities and results, prior to making important decisions. Imagining your life like a movie helps you see your destination more clearly and hopefully helps you avoid mistakes.

Fast-forward your life. Play the movie.

Playing the movie means asking the question, "If I change nothing, what situation will I be in five years from now?"

By doing this, instead of living out *more* pain, you're just borrowing pain from your future and adding it to today's pain. When you peer into your future and see your situation is worse, it motivates you to say, "That is enough!" That realization puts you over the top so you say, "That's it. I don't like where I'm headed. I'm willing to change today so that five years from now, I'll be in a better position."

Change Begins Now

Making this kind of decision is huge, but real change happens when you start paying the price. Everything in life has a price tag. Making your payments is painful. It is difficult. However, you must go through it to end up where you want to be five years from now, miles ahead of your current situation.

In order to do this—to be able to experience God's best—you have to admit that you have previously (and currently) been willing to settle for less. You can't get to *more* until you admit that you are living *less*. It's time to own up to your mistakes, to admit where you are right now. God wants to bring powerful changes to our lives, but we must allow Him.

There is no better time to realize where you are than right now. Don't waste another day settling for less than God's best. It is time to commit to breaking the cycle of failure. Bear in mind, the Israelites were living in the Promised Land, yet they were living far below their promise. Don't let this be your future.

Looking Back–Looking Forward

This book wasn't written to take up space or fill up your time, but rather to be a tool for changing your life.

Do you want to change? Do you want more out of life? If so, get ready to grow far beyond anything you thought possible.

Start by learning the first lessons:

- Recognize your cycle of failure.

- Realize what has been causing you pain.

- Don't run from the pain—experience it.

- Make a decision to change.

- Begin to change right now.

ACTION PLAN

What areas in your life do you need to look at and ask, "Where am I, and where do I want to *be* in five years?" Maybe your greatest challenges are in the area of finances or in your career. Perhaps it is your marriage or your relationships. Maybe it is depression or addiction. I don't know what it is for you. Maybe it is none of those things but something totally different.

I want to do a little exercise with you, to give you a little more pain, to bring you to the threshold of *change*. For this exercise and the rest of the exercises in the book, get out that notebook I mentioned previously.

Try to imagine yourself five years from now. Imagine the problems that you're currently going through as we focus on the pain in your life. After you've taken some time to think about it, write down your answers to the following questions:

1. What is causing you the greatest pain today? Do your best to describe what that pain feels like.

2. With that pain (and its causes) in mind, if nothing changes, what will that pain (and your life) be like five years from now?

3. If you are able to change things and rid yourself of the cause of your pain, what will your life be like five years from now? Where will you be?

If you want to change, if you want to discover and experience God's best, commit to finishing this book. Commit to working through the exercises and applying the truths that we will discover in the following chapters.

Please stop reading for a moment, spend a little time in prayer, and tell God that you are ready to change.

THE angel of the LORD came and sat down under the oak in Ophrah that belonged to Joash the Abiezrite, where his son Gideon was threshing wheat in a winepress to keep it from the Midianites. When the angel of the LORD appeared to Gideon, he said, "The LORD is with you, mighty warrior."

(JUDGES 6:11–12)

STEP TWO

Mighty warrior"?

It's not hard to imagine what Gideon must have thought when he heard the angel say those words. At that moment Gideon and his countrymen were overwhelmed with trouble. Israel, the once-proud and powerful nation, had been reduced to little more than beggars who hid in caves. They had been openly humiliated by the Midianites and other eastern tribes who came and took whatever they wanted.

When the angel of the Lord found Gideon, he was threshing wheat—separating the grain from the chaff—at the bottom of a winepress so he could make food for his family.

Normally, you would thresh wheat in a high place called a threshing floor, where there would be plenty of wind to blow away the chaff. But Gideon was threshing in a winepress, down in a valley. The process was much less effective in the valley, but consider what drove him there. Gideon was afraid of the Midianites, scared that they were going to chase him down and take his food. Give him credit for being industrious, but the scene described in Judges 6 is sad. Gideon was a young man from a small town, the runt of the family, hiding in a winepress, trying to get enough grain winnowed to make food. He was focused on that day's lunch.

And at that moment an angel of the Lord showed up.

As soon as the angel appeared, questions erupted from Gideon's heart. He was just like the rest of us. We think we are weak, even when God sees us as strong.

"Why do you call me a mighty warrior?"

It is obvious that Gideon didn't feel like a mighty warrior. He was filled with embittered questions:

> "But sir," Gideon replied, "if the LORD is with us, why has all this happened to us? Where are all his wonders that our fathers told us about when they said, 'Did not the LORD bring us up out of Egypt?' But now the LORD has abandoned us and put us into the hand of Midian." (Judges 6:13)

God's chosen people had turned their backs on Him and gone into open and depraved idolatry (Judges 6:1). But when God delivered them into the hands of the Midianites for seven years, many people throughout Israel reached their threshold of pain and started crying out for God's deliverance (Judges 6:7). God answered those pleas by sending the angel to call Gideon to do the impossible.

The conversation between the angel and Gideon took a serious turn quickly.

"Go save Israel!"

The angel arrived with a message direct from the throne room of heaven. The messenger came with the authority given by God. It was the angel of the Lord, but even more, it was God's *presence* in the form of an angel.

In fact, in Judges 6:14, the Hebrew word *Lord* is actually "Jehovah," for the angel spoke as one having God's authority, not as a mere messenger.

> "Never tell a young person that something can't be done. God may have waited centuries for someone ignorant enough of the impossible to do that very thing."
>
> — MICHAEL LEBOEUF

Imagine Gideon's reaction. A message delivered by an angel! It was as if God Himself had shown up there at the winepress as Gideon hid from the Midianites. What happened in the next few moments would change an entire nation, and it would all take place because of God's call upon an unlikely leader.

> "The five happiest people I have ever met all had this strange little quirk of referring to their jobs as a 'calling.'"
>
> — ERIC SEVAREID

Does this sound familiar? Do you find yourself asking, "That's great for Gideon or some big-time minister, but what does this mean for me?" God often specializes in breaking through with a startling divine message and calling unlikely people to impossible tasks, even though they have questions, doubts, insecurities, and checkered pasts.

A Divine Appointment

Some people today might look at this situation—an angel showing up as God's empowered representative to talk with Gideon—and get a little frustrated. It is easy to sit back and say, "It must be nice. When is an angel going to show up for *me*? When are some cherubim going to show up at the end of *my* bed and give *me* some directions? I'll take an e-mail, a note, something... *anything*!" It is easy to see what happened to Gideon and say, "I could follow God too, if an angel showed up and talked to *me*." Sometimes we use that as an excuse.

I hear people asking why there are so many angelic appearances in the Bible. Let's take a deeper look at what was actually going on. Whenever an angel shows up in Scripture, it's for a specific purpose. In this case, Israel was running out of options. The Midianites and eastern tribes were closing in on the children of Israel. God's chosen people were slated to be annihilated.

Angelic appearances and miracles seem to occur whenever God is getting ready to reveal Himself to people who don't know Him or who have forgotten Him. Time and again, when you see incredible miracles happen in the Bible, they are usually clustered around the introduction of God to a new group of people whom He wants to use, people who previously knew nothing about God, or people who have ignored Him for a long period of time. This is what happened in the book of Judges.

Of all people, why did the angel of the Lord appear to Gideon? Gideon himself is quick to point out that he is the least in a family that is among the least in the land. Despite that fact, God's call on Gideon to save Israel from its enemies is consistent with the rest of Scripture:

> "There's an old expression, 'Seeing is believing.' But it's more accurate to say that 'believing is seeing.' That is, you tend to see what you believe you're going to see. You bring to a situation what you expect you're going to experience."
>
> — CARL SORENSEN, PHD

But God chose the foolish things of
the world to shame the wise; God chose the weak things of the world to shame the strong. He chose the lowly things of this world and the despised things—and the things that are not—to nullify the things that are, so that no one may boast before him. (1 Corinthians 1:27–29)

When the angel said to Gideon in Judges 6:12, "The LORD is with you, mighty warrior," there was nothing close to heroic about Gideon's character. Gideon was weak and insignificant. It was as if the angel had walked up to a ninety-eight-pound weakling and said, "Hey, big guy, let's go win an impossible war!" God was speaking truth into

Gideon—not current truth, but *future* truth. God doesn't speak to us as we *are*.

Self-Sufficiency

Another reason God decided to send an angel to present the call to Gideon seems to be rooted in the fact that Gideon had no other resources or advisors who could have poured courage and commitment into his life.

Gideon had none of the resources we have available today. He didn't have the completed Word of God. He didn't have *anyone* speaking truth to him.

So God sent an angel.

Imagine what would have happened had Gideon decided to fight the Midianites on his own. If Gideon had said, "You know, I'll go talk to my dad about doing God's will. He can give me some advice."

Problem was, his dad wasn't following God.

Could Gideon have talked to his mom, his brothers, or his sisters about the need to follow God and stand against the Midianites? Nope. None of them were following God either.

> God speaks to us as He knows we can *become.*

"I know," Gideon might have said. "I'll talk to an old school buddy." Nope. No one was serving God. They had all joined the other side, the side of the idol worshippers.

"Maybe I'll talk to some wise man in town or another region of the country."

No one in the next town or the next. No one anywhere, for that matter. The entire nation had turned its back on God. According to Judges 6, other than a prophet mentioned in the early part of Gideon's story, there wasn't a single person, purpose, or truth to be found. Nowhere!

Thankfully, in God's providence, when you have no person, purpose, or truth from God anywhere around you, as in Gideon's case, He sends an angel.

This does not mean that God doesn't want us to lean on advisors. But when there are no advisors to speak of, God will speak directly to you. Sometimes this will happen through His Word, sometimes through the Holy Spirit, and sometimes through an over-whelming desire that comes upon you. This may even happen during a season of solitude, when God has your undivided attention and can speak most clearly to you.

> "If you have something exciting, a goal that you really care about, you don't have to be pushed; the vision pulls you."
>
> — STEVE JOBS

Why don't we see angels and the miraculous in our lives today? For starters, God has already given us something far more practical. He has given His Word. In addition, God has already placed amazing resources all around you. There are hundreds of books collecting dust at your local bookstore, books that could show you how to achieve more in any number of areas in your life. There are dozens of conferences, Web sites, audio books, CDs, DVDs, and MP3s, all devoted to helping you discover God's best for your life.

Not only that, but there are people all around you who are follow-ing God and have already achieved much in the area where you want to excel. Are you willing to call them? Are you willing to listen?

You probably aren't going to get an angel of the Lord or a miracle until you have exhausted all the resources at your disposal. God sends miracles when there's nothing left, when we're out of options, because God will *never* reward our laziness.

In any case, you probably don't need an angel. You may just need a book, a course, a class, or a mentor. The book of Proverbs tells us, "Whoever walks with the wise becomes wise" (Proverbs 13:20, NRSV).

You may already know someone who can give you advice, someone who has what you want, someone who has found God's best in an area of his or her life in which you have similar dreams.

> "Humility is a magnet for the Holy Spirit."
>
> — RICK WARREN

What is keeping you from calling them?

Could it be pride? Apathy? Maybe you're just overthinking the issue.

Pride keeps us from admitting the truth that we might not be strong in our marriage, our finances, our parenting, or our spiritual walk. Humility, on the other hand, makes us open to new ideas, new concepts, and new ways of doing things. Humility is not about being quiet, reticent, or inactive. Instead, it's about seeing our shortcomings, taking steps to overcome them, and changing our actions to create a new future.

Why Gideon?

After everything that had happened, after everything they had lost, the Israelites still turned away from God. Only one person was willing to listen to God's voice—Gideon. He was a man who was uniquely called by God to face a challenge that no one else could—or would— face.

When the angel of the Lord found Gideon, he was threshing wheat at the bottom of a winepress. He was separating it from the chaff so he could make food. As I mentioned earlier, it was common practice in Gideon's day to thresh wheat at the top of a mountain or hill. At the bottom of the mountain they would have a winepress, a place to collect and crush grapes to make wine.

Gideon was threshing wheat not at the top of the mountain but down at the bottom in the winepress. He was hiding from the Midianites, trying to thresh the wheat, but probably to no avail since there was no wind at the base of the mountain. Also, the Bible tells us that Gideon was trying to thresh the wheat with a staff or rod, probably because he had so little. He obviously didn't have enough to require oxen or a larger instrument.

He was in a poor location, trying to make it work because he was afraid to go up to the top of the mountain. Gideon was afraid that the Midianites would spot him, then chase him down and take his food. He was a young man from a small town, the runt of the family, trying to make his lunch when an angel of the Lord shows up.

At least he was working and busy—he wasn't lazy. He had servants (Judges 6:27), but he was threshing wheat. Gideon wasn't living in idleness or hiding out in the caves, sulking because he and his family had nothing to eat. He was hiding from the Midianites, but at least he kept trying to do something.

God gives divine visits to people who are seeking and working. Shepherds received tidings of Christ's birth while they were keeping their flocks.

In the midst of working, despite his distress, Gideon received a calling from God's angel.

■ Your Calling

Over the years I have been an ardent student of what works and why some people, like Gideon, overcome incredible odds to succeed in doing the "impossible." Here are ten of the most common traits of those who experience God's best:

THEY RECOGNIZE AND FOLLOW GOD'S CALL

First, let's define what we mean by "God's call."

Sometimes the call of God can be very specific, as in a call to missionary service or ministry, or in Gideon's case, a call to defeat

> "A single idea can transform a life, a business, a nation, a world."
>
> — DAN ZADRA

an enemy. However, throughout this book I'll be using the phrase "God's call" or "calling" in a broader sense. When I refer to finding and following God's calling for your life, I'm referring to discovering God's direction for your life. Sometimes we describe this as seeking God's will for our lives. That's what change is all about: discovering and following God's direction—God's best—for our lives.

So how do you recognize God's call? How do you know what He's directing you to do? Listen for God's voice. Study the Bible, seek the Holy Spirit's direction, ask the counsel of godly people, pray earnestly, and then obey with an unshakable faith.

Even if you have a tough time nailing it down, be assured that God has a divine calling upon your life. And keep in mind that a calling to business or education can be just as significant as a call to be a missionary, provided that the calling is from the Lord. What's important is that in whatever you're doing, you are following God's leadership and direction.

Romans 12:2 gives us the long and short of it: "Do not conform any longer to the pattern of this world, but be transformed by the renewing of your mind. Then you will be able to test and approve what God's will is—his good, pleasing and perfect will."

THEY HAVE AN UNSHAKABLE VISION

Everyone called to the work of the Lord faces challenges. People throughout the Old and New Testaments did. Gideon certainly did, as we will see in the forthcoming chapters. All the pioneers of the faith did.

So will you.

Once you know God's will, you must pursue it with an unshakable vision and faith. There will be people who doubt you, your vision, and your ability to accomplish it. But rather than being discouraged by those people and their skepticism, you should let those doubts increase your resolve and your determination to move forward and be successful.

The truth is, when you know where God is leading you, you will find a way to follow. God will provide the strength and the means. Make sure that your vision is unshakable.

THEY DEMONSTRATE DEPENDENCE UPON GOD, YET INDEPENDENCE FROM MAN

Even though most successful believers can work within the constraints of organization, teamwork, and a shared vision, the best ones also have an independent streak. This usually causes them to be more innovative and creative than people who prefer "going with the flow." They are dependent on God but demonstrate a certain independence from other people. Sometimes they're described as "mavericks."

Look at the leaders throughout the Bible and follow their example. You'll see that many of them (Daniel, for one) demonstrate this independent streak. However, keep in mind that, even if you are a maverick, you need to be able to work well with those around you. Most firings are due to an inability to work with others. If you are to be a leader and innovator, you need to be able to get your ideas across without becoming a threat to those around you. For example, if you come up with a new idea in your work-

> "As long as I have to die my own death, I have decided to live my own life and not let others live it for me."
>
> — HANOCH MCCARTY

place, you might want to present it in such a way that your employer can take credit for it. President Harry S. Truman is reported to have said, "It's amazing what you can accomplish if you don't care who gets the credit."

Learn to work well with others as both leader and follower. But in the end, remember that you must depend ultimately upon God for guidance and direction.

THEY ARE WILLING TO WORK HARD

There is simply nothing that takes the place of hard work. Gideon was found faithful, threshing wheat, when the angel of the Lord appeared to him with a divine calling.

You should count the costs, of course, and plan well. Yet in the end, unless you have an appetite for hard work, you probably won't succeed.

There may be exceptions, but I haven't met any. Most people who succeed in any area are those who find a way to get things done, who don't stop working just because it is five o'clock in the afternoon and everyone else has gone home. Most of the great leaders that I know and have known have started out working long and hard hours with little pay other than the reward of doing what God directed them to do.

> "Things do not change; we change."
>
> — HENRY DAVID THOREAU

And when success comes, these same great ones find a way to stay motivated, to continue to work harder than others, and to never rest on their laurels. Anything less doesn't seem to work.

THEY POSSESS A DEEP INNER CONFIDENCE

You might call it self-confidence, but with believers that assurance and belief must come from God Himself. As with Gideon, there will be times that you must get alone and find out what God's plan is for your life. Your deepening confidence in the Lord will help you succeed when all else fails.

Six or seven years ago our church was facing a good problem. We had reached all of our goals in only three years instead of the ten we thought it would take. I didn't know where we should go next, so I sought the Lord and asked Him what to do.

I felt Him leading me to pray more.

"How much more?" I asked. "A few days? Weeks?"

Ultimately, I felt the Lord leading me to commit to praying one hundred hours about the future vision and direction of Bay Area Fellowship. I announced my plan to the church, and they held me accountable. So, over the next two to three months, I spent a hundred hours in prayer for our church's vision. What resulted was a quiet confidence in God's direction and leading for the future.

This time in prayer also gave me assurance when people expressed doubts about that vision. I was able to gently ask them how much they had prayed about it. Now, it wasn't my intent to one-up people in prayer, but by spending that time with God, I had developed confidence in what He was leading us to do. I was better able to challenge the church to get on board.

We tend to take the side of the person we spend the most time with. If you spend time with God, you're going to take His side.

THEY MAJOR ON THE MAJORS, NOT ON THE MINORS

Successful people like Gideon are people who resist the temptation to do what is unimportant or easiest; instead, they seem to have the innate ability to spotlight the essentials—the task at hand. They have the ability to get up in the morning and tackle the most important goal of the day without getting sidetracked. They have the ability to turn off the phone and the e-mail, to close the door of their office, to focus on what needs to be done.

In order to develop this ability, you need to keep your vision and goals before you all the time. One way to do this, when you get alone with the Lord to pray, is to repeatedly ask yourself, "What do I want?" I believe that—if we're spending time with God as we should—He often reveals His will for us through our desires. Many people are unhappy

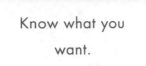

Know what you want.

not because they don't have what they want but because they don't even *know* what they want.

When it's all said and done, and you're lying in a casket, what do you want to have accomplished? What do you want to be true about your life? Keeping those desires focused and clear in your mind is how you learn to major on the majors, not on the minors.

THEY EXERCISE SOUND JUDGMENT

People who experience God's best seem to have the ability to think quickly, process alternatives rapidly, and somehow come to wise decisions even under the greatest pressure.

In fact, people like Gideon have an ability to overcome all the odds, almost without exception, by making stress work for them.

Wisdom, especially under pressure, comes from God. More importantly, it comes from a deepening, intimate relationship with Him. There is only one way to obtain wise, sound judgment—to spend time with God, listening to Him.

I've always been very numbers-oriented in my goals for Bay Area Fellowship. In my planning, I had specific numerical goals for where the church should be at certain times. But a little over a year ago, I felt God leading me to forget about the numbers for a while and instead focus on prayer. So I decided to set a personal goal for prayer. I made the commitment to pray for two hours every day and also asked for two thousand people from our church to commit to praying one hour each week for a year. That way, we would have one hundred thousand hours of prayer devoted to the mission of Bay Area Fellowship.

God provided those people, and in that single year of prayer—not focusing on numerical growth—Bay Area Fellowship became one of the fastest-growing churches in the United States and also one of the largest churches in the country.

THEY HAVE A CHANGE-FRIENDLY ATTITUDE

As we will see with Gideon, one of the greatest traits of those who seek God's best and follow His leading is the ability to accept change, even to embrace it. Change occurs frequently in life and in battles, and those who succeed seem to thrive on changes as their opportunities and resources grow. Gideon and his warriors did. So can you.

Later in this book we'll see how Gideon goes from a small army of 32,000 to a tiny army of 10,000, and finally to a relative handful of soldiers—only 300. On top of that, the battle strategy is not to fight but instead to stand on top of a hill with trumpets, torches, and clay pots.

Can you imagine being Gideon? God asks you to take on a massive, intimidating enemy with a microscopic army whose equipment consists of little more than trumpets and Tupperware. But Gideon was able to accept that change because he knew his God and he had a clear vision of what God intended to do.

The clearer your vision is, the easier it will be to accept change.

THEY TAKE RESPONSIBILITY FOR THEIR CHOICES

Discovering and experiencing God's best is no accident, just as success in any endeavor is no accident. Likewise, failure is no accident. Success and failure are directly related to our choices and actions.

As we will see in the next chapter, people like Gideon learned to take responsibility for their choices—past, present, and future. In fact, assuming responsibility for those decisions is liberating beyond measure when it comes to following God's direction for your life.

> "The spirit of venture is lost in the inertia of a mind against change."
> — ALFRED P. SLOAN

God gives us great freedom to choose. Of course, He doesn't want us to sin or to resist His will. In fact, it is imperative that we make choices that are in agreement with His will. But how do you know?

Walking closely with the Lord is a prerequisite. So is desiring His will for yourself and the people whom you serve. Then God will place His desires in your heart, for the Word of God declares, "Delight yourself in the LORD and he will give you the desires of your heart" (Psalm 37:4). The key is to seek God's will, not your own.

Learn to pursue God's guidance, but don't blame Him for your bad decisions. Sometimes you will make great decisions; sometimes you won't. Bad choices help you learn to listen more closely so that you can make better choices. Taking responsibility for your choices is one of the major keys to your future ability to grow and experience nothing less than God's best.

THEY KEEP THEIR EYES ON THE PRIZE

It is important to manage the everyday details, certainly, but the mundane can often bog you down unless you find a way to focus consistently on the end result, not just the process of getting there.

For Gideon, that end result was leading his warrior band to victory. For us today, that end result should certainly include leading others to know Christ and helping them to come into the abundant life. Beyond those ideals, however, is an even more important prize that we must keep in mind—standing someday before God and hearing Him say, "Well done, good and faithful servant . . . enter thou into the joy of thy lord" (Matthew 25:23, KJV).

What a wonderful, eternal prize! And what an overriding reason to always seek God's best.

▬ Looking Back–Looking Forward

Where we start is not important; it is where we finish that makes the difference. God doesn't speak to us as we *are*. He speaks to us as we can become. God separates us from our current failures, our current situations, so we look at ourselves as winners.

In Gideon, God created something totally different from what had been. He'll do that for you too. He is leading you today to follow a better path. With that comes the commitment to help you accomplish what He wants you to do. "The one who calls you is faithful and he will do it" (I Thessalonians 5:24).

How do we find and follow God's leading? Begin by seeking to understand the following words:

> So do not worry, saying, "What shall we eat?" or "What shall we drink?" or "What shall we wear?" For the pagans run after all these things, and your heavenly Father knows that you need them. But seek first his kingdom and his righteousness, and all these things will be given to you as well. (Matthew 6:31–33)

We know from God's Word and Gideon's life that He cares about the things that concern us and the decisions, both huge and small, we face every day. He understands what makes us tick, and He knows our needs. He knows how to help us follow His direction in our lives, whether we are facing the Midianites, as Gideon did, or our own everyday challenges.

Likewise, He cares about the choices we must make: "For this God is our God for ever and ever; he will be our guide even to the end" (Psalm 48:14).

Most important, He wants us to make decisions that reflect His will in our lives: "Therefore do not be foolish, but understand what the Lord's will is" (Ephesians 5:17). With these verses in mind, here are three quick principles for knowing God's plan in your life:

1. God's plan is available today only through the Lord Jesus Christ. While the world seeks guidance through a smorgasbord of beliefs and rituals, Jesus proclaims Himself in a clear-cut way that leaves no room for error or misinterpretation; "Jesus answered, 'I am the way and the truth and the life. No one comes to the Father except through me'" (John 14:6).

2. To know God's will in your life, you must first offer your life to God. The Apostle Paul wrote, "Therefore, I urge you, brothers, in view of God's mercy, to offer your bodies as living sacrifices, holy and pleasing to God—this is your spiritual act of worship" (Romans 12:1). We must be willing to be living sacrifices before we can be used by Him as a reasonable service. Only then can we begin to understand His design for our lives. If you have never asked Jesus Christ into your life, you can pray this simple prayer and know for sure you will go to heaven one day because of what Jesus did for you on the cross:

> Dear Jesus, I believe You died for my sins. You paid the price I owe for what I've done that dishonors You. I believe You died and rose again from the grave, proving You are God. I turn from my sins, and I invite You into my life. Be my Lord, my eternal Savior. I put You in charge. In Jesus' name, amen.

3. To know God's will, your mind must be renewed supernaturally. As mentioned, the book of Romans tells us, "Do not conform any longer to the pattern of this world, but be transformed by the renewing of your mind. Then you will be able to test and approve what God's will is—his good, pleasing and perfect will" (Romans 12:2). As we consistently present ourselves to God by spending time with Him and reading His Word, then He can transform and show us His plan.

God's plan for your life is perfect and complete. He seeks to bring each believer into His perfect will. As we seek to know His will for our lives, we must pray with the psalmist, "Teach me to do your will, for you are my God; may your good Spirit lead me on level ground" (Psalm 143:10).

ACTION PLAN

In Step 1, I asked you to think about the questions: "Where am I, and where do I want to *be* in five years?" I also asked you to write your responses in a notebook. Now, open your notebook and review your answers. Then answer the following questions on a new page.

1. As you have sought God's guidance for those questions, has your answer changed? If so, how?

2. What are the biggest obstacles that keep you from accomplishing what God wants you to do in your life?

3. Now take a few moments to reflect on how you feel about your answers. What do your sentences say about your hopes for the future? What are the implications? What kind of person holds these kinds of hopes?

THE LORD answered, "I will be with you, and you will strike down all the Midianites together." Gideon replied, "If now I have found favor in your eyes, give me a sign that it is really you talking to me. Please do not go away until I come back and bring my offering and set it before you." And the LORD said, "I will wait until you return."

(JUDGES 6:16–18)

STEP THREE

Everything in life has a price tag. Real change happens when you start paying the price. For Gideon, this meant setting aside his excuses, coming to grips with his past, and making a commitment to move forward.

"Okay," Gideon finally said to the angel, "I get it. I need a sign that this is for real. Let me go get an offering."

There in that winepress, Gideon made a conscious decision to change. Making the kind of decision Gideon made is huge, and its implications are far-reaching. Paying the price of change is painful and difficult. However, you must go through it to end up where you want to be five years from now, miles ahead of your current situation.

So, what did Gideon have to do in order to change his (and his nation's) life?

First, he had to come to grips with his current situation. In order to discover God's best for your life, you have to admit that you have been settling for less. You can't get to more until you admit that you are living less. Gideon kept asking questions:

"But LORD," Gideon asked, "how can I save Israel? My clan is the weakest in Manasseh, and I am the least in my family." The LORD answered, "I will be with you, and you will strike down all the Midianites together" (Judges 6:15–16).

43

In Gideon's case, he finally had to admit where he was—where Israel was—before he could change himself and eventually lead the entire nation to a glorious victory. He had to let go of his excuses.

God spoke to him and delivered him in a powerful way. He gave Gideon the strategic steps to bring incredible victory, completely transforming his life economically, emotionally, spiritually, and relationally. In the end, Gideon truly became a "mighty warrior," transformed in every possible way.

It is time to own up to your mistakes, to admit where you are right now. Only then can God do something great and miraculous with your life. There is no better time to realize where you are than right now. Don't waste another day settling for less than God's best. Remember, the Israelites were living in the Promised Land, yet they were living far below their potential. Don't let this be your future.

Also, keep in mind that Gideon went through a process in which he learned that the cost of following God's leading would be high, that there would be a price to pay. There will be a price for you to pay too.

Set Aside Your Excuses

As humans, we always want to blame other things, other people, other factors; but God always turns it back on us. He never lets us play the blame game because He knows that our future is dependent upon our actions. When we are in a crisis, in a painful situation that reaches our threshold of pain, God says, "Let's talk about *you*."

Naturally, we are quick to answer like Gideon. God tells him that he's a mighty warrior, but Gideon replies, "No, no, no, I want to talk about the Midianites."

God responds, "No, let's talk about you."

"But the Midianites are mean."

> "You can't escape the responsibility of tomorrow by evading it today."
>
> — ABRAHAM LINCOLN

God says, "That's because you're *letting* them be mean, because you haven't put your foot down and haven't done what I have told you to do."

God knows that we can only be treated as well or as poorly as we allow others to treat us. The Israelites could have stopped their enemies. They could have demanded an end to the injustices. Yet, because they felt weak and powerless, the Children of Promise allowed themselves to be treated poorly. They let the Midianites walk all over them, stealing their crops, their sheep, and their donkeys!

How often do we complain, "There's a person at work who is running over me. I'm going to quit my job and go work somewhere else. Maybe they won't have any mean people there"? Do you see the problem here? Whom do we need to face at the office? Whom do we really need to confront? The person we need to confront is ourself. We must pay the price of self-discovery.

Pain has a way of making us face ourselves. Outward difficulties are really just internal battles for courage, the courage to face our own fears. We have to face ourselves and our own lack of assertiveness.

Before he could lead the Israelites, Gideon first had to take responsibility for himself and his fears. Likewise, there is only one person you are "response-able" for—and that is *you*. If you really want to change, you have to stop playing the victim and start taking responsibility for yourself, for the direction you allow your life to go. Israel had become a nation of victims, but because one man was willing to face his fears, everything was about to change:

> "But sir," Gideon replied, "if the LORD is with us, why has all this happened to us? Where are all his wonders that our fathers told us about when they said, 'Did not the LORD bring us up out of Egypt?' But now the LORD has abandoned us and put us into the hand of Midian." (Judges 6:13)

I think it's interesting at this point to see that Gideon is serving up a really big excuse. God said, "Hey, mighty hero, welcome. Glad you're here. I've got some things for you to do." And Gideon said, "Wait a minute. Why is all this bad stuff happening?" Now before you look down on Gideon, keep in mind all of the excuses that we give God.

Gideon asked a classic question that most people ask at one time or another. "Why do bad things happen to good people?" This is many people's standard excuse for not trusting God. If God really cares about us, why does He let sorrow and difficulties come into our lives?

> "A new philosophy, a way of life, is not given for nothing. It has to be paid dearly for and only acquired with much patience and great effort."
>
> — FYODOR DOSTOYEVSKY

I want to break that question down into its basic assumptions. When we ask why bad things happen to us, we're assuming that everything is always supposed to go our way. We reason that as long as we're nice people, life shouldn't have any rough spots. Bad things—tragedy and trials—shouldn't happen to us. But when we think that way we're forgetting that we live in an evil, fallen world. Bad things happen all the time, and God's people aren't exempt.

If we live long enough, we all will live with a lot of heartache. Sadly, that's just part of life. In order to experience God's best, we must face our fears. We must face the fact that life can be frightening because bad things happen.

Face Your Fears

The Greek word for fear is *phobos*. This word has within its meaning ideas such as flight, dread, terror, and to be intimidated by an enemy. Satan is fully aware of what fear means. He is the enemy of our lives, and he wants us to live in such fear that we cannot operate in faith. He loves to see us react without faith to the situations, challenges, and obstacles that come our way daily. When we react in fear rather than faith, we fall right into his trap. We run from our problems and circumstances, whether figuratively or literally, and we forget that we are endowed with faith from our Creator.

> No matter what you believe, you always have been and always will be the product of your choices.

Fear is the opposite of faith.

As with Gideon, your future depends upon the way you respond to the information you receive every day, as well as the calling God has placed upon your life. The same God who spoke the universe into existence sees what you're dealing with now. He envisioned our earth for our benefit and enjoyment. He knows our needs, our wants, our desires, and our fears. And he wants us to experience a full, abundant life.

Your desire for happiness, money, marriage, children, business, and health all depend on your ability to begin unleashing the dreams He has placed within you. Everything you need is available for your future if you will see what God already sees, especially since He created you to achieve at a level beyond anything you ever dreamed possible.

No matter what you believe, you always have been and always will be the product of your choices. When choices are based on traditional concepts that dictate that risk is bad and failure is shameful, we choose to avoid risk and failure. And if we avoid risk and failure, we simultaneously avoid success. We adopt mediocre lifestyles, and we become mediocre people.

Mediocrity is what life is all about for some people. But it doesn't have to be that way. If boring, complacent lifestyles are the result of our choices, then fulfilling, exciting lifestyles can just as easily be ours. It's all a matter of what choices we're willing to make and the risks we're willing to take.

And make no mistake, the choice is yours.

This book is about growth and making faith-filled decisions, just as Gideon did. It is about taking responsibility for failure and success, just as Gideon did. What choices are you willing to make?

Look at two of God's creatures—the oyster and the eagle. Immediately after birth, the oyster is set for life. It lives in its own shell, which protects it from predators. When it desires food, it only has to open its shell and filter the nourishment contained in seawater. The eagle, on the other hand, operates under a different set of circumstances. It must work for all it obtains. It must build its own nest and endure snow, ice, wind, and rain to find food.

But there's another side to this story. The oyster pays dearly for its security. Its protective shell is also its prison. Oysters also have no means of defense. This makes oysters easy prey for people who take grand delight in cracking open their shells, splashing them with a shot of Tabasco, and letting them slide—alive and helpless—down their throats.

Sure, an oyster has it easy. But who wants to be an oyster?

How about the eagle? It is not imprisoned. Its almost-limitless confines are God's blue sky. It is not defenseless. With wings that can propel it to amazing altitudes and talons that can repel even the most vicious of predators, eagles are a rarity on any creature's menu.

> "Don't be afraid to take a large step if one is indicated. You can't cross a chasm in two small jumps."
>
> — DAVID LLOYD GEORGE

Because of its strength and ability to maintain independence, one of these creatures has become the symbol of America and freedom. The eagle takes responsibility for its life because it must. Human beings, on the other hand, have choices.

Sure, people can choose to be oysters. The world is full of people who have shifted responsibility for their lives to their family, friends, their company or government. And as long as others willingly assume that responsibility, these people will continue to act irresponsibly. Of course, if friends and relatives refuse to accept this responsibility, these people— like oysters—find themselves at the mercy of the forces that surround them.

> "It costs so much to be a full human being that there are very few who have the enlightenment or the courage to pay the price."
>
> – MORRIS L. WEST, *THE SHOES OF A FISHERMAN*

But people can also choose to be eagles if they dare. True, being responsible is not always easy. Sometimes it is downright difficult and taxing to both body and soul. But there are great rewards. Eagles fly as high as they like. And they don't slide down the throats of anyone or anything.

In short, finding God's best means facing our fears and taking responsibility for our choices.

Gideon did, and you can too!

Following God's Leading Requires Commitment

Even in the midst of Gideon's questions and doubts, the angel told him, "Go in the strength you have and save Israel out of Midian's hand. Am I not sending you?" (Judges 6:14).

At some point, we must understand that obeying God's direction requires commitment on our part. All too often we want God to give us supernatural help and He is asking us to use our "natural" resources first. When we see supernatural events happen it's because God adds His "super" to our natural.

It's ironic, isn't it? We keep waiting for God to do some huge and miraculous thing, yet God is waiting for us to do something un-miraculous. He's waiting for us to get moving.

God says to Gideon, "Am I not sending you? Didn't I tell you to do this? Gideon, go with the strength and the ability you already have."

Gideon's response was much as ours would be in the same situation: "But *Lord*, Gideon asked, how can I save Israel? My clan is the weakest in Manasseh and I am the least in my family" (Judges 6:15). In other words, "You want little old weak me to do something about the Midianites?"

Most of us live with an inferiority complex. We don't think we can accomplish anything. We don't think we're of great value. We think we come from the worst side of the tracks, the wrong family, the wrong pedigree, the wrong town, the wrong skin color, the wrong socioeconomic class. We think we have all these things against us, when in reality God wants to use us in an amazing way right where we are.

> "It's never going to get better than it is now. You've just got to keep trying; when it's easy, you're dead."
>
> — JOHN H. JOHNSON, FOUNDER, *EBONY* MAGAZINE

We think God can't use us because we don't have enough strength. In fact—as we'll see later in this book—often the very reason God doesn't use a person is because he or she has *too much* strength.

So the Lord answered, "I will be with you, and you will strike down all the Midianites together" (Judges 6:16).

Have you noticed that there are two different conversations going on here? Gideon brings up excuses and complaints, but God doesn't answer any of those. God keeps saying, "Here's what I want you to do. Go in your strength. Go in your power. I want you to do what I say, deliver yourself and all your people from the Midianites."

A lot of times we say, "God is not speaking to me. I'm asking, but He won't give me answers." Maybe the reason God's not answering you is because you're not asking the right questions. God does not want us to wallow in self-centered requests that are suited for failure. He wants us to focus our attention—and our prayers—on His purposes, His concerns, His directives.

And when God's call comes, we need to commit ourselves to following it. Following God requires absolute commitment.

Here is why: Commitment strengthens our resolve during difficult times.

When I go to an amusement park, I'm never told at the gate, "Now look, you have to be really committed to being here. We know it's going to be tough, but try to stay committed to having fun all day." No one ever has to say that to me. You know why? It doesn't require commitment because it's always fun.

> "Take charge of your thoughts."
>
> — PLATO

On the other hand, when a man and woman get married, we ask for a lifelong commitment. Why? Every marriage has tough seasons. It requires commitment to get through those times.

That is part of paying the price. It is part of the equation. Not to feel the need for commitment means that you don't anticipate any problems. That is unrealistic. But to ask for a commitment assumes that there will be difficult times ahead. When God asks for your commitment, He wants you to be prepared for the tough times. If you understand that built in to the very word *commitment* is the idea of rough spots ahead, then you will be ready to follow His lead and experience His best for you.

So be willing to pay the price as you follow God by making a commitment as Gideon did. You are going to walk with God through some experiences that you may not understand. There may be times when everything goes wrong. To respond to God with commitment means that you will trust Him even when things are bad, when circumstances don't meet your expectations, when hardships come, and when life is not fair. Whatever problems you face, you choose to follow God anyway.

If you're waiting on God to improve your situation, you might be surprised to find that God's really waiting on *you*. God tells us, "I love you and I am with you. Now trust Me and move forward."

God loves us right where we are, but He loves us too much to let us stay there. He wants to transform us and to deliver us out of the messes and mediocrity we create. He loves us so much that He wants to bring real change into our lives, just as He did with Gideon.

Sealing the Commitment

Gideon viewed himself as a failure, as someone who would never achieve anything. But God said, "Gideon, go on your own strength." That is exactly what Gideon began to do. Immediately he began to pay the price. Gideon said, "If now I have found favor in your eyes, give me a sign that it is really you talking to me. Please do not go away until I come back and bring my offering and set it before you" (Judges 6:17–18).

Gideon felt the need to make a sacrifice to God to seal his calling. Whenever God uses someone in a big way, he asks that person to sacrifice. No matter what story you go to in the Bible, you will find that before God uses people to do great things, He requires them to make a sacrifice.

"In life you are either serving a purpose, or you are just serving time."

— VIC CONANT, PRESIDENT, NIGHTINGALE-CONANT

The reasons are clear: God uses givers, not takers. God will not develop you to your full potential if you are primarily a taker.

The Bible is filled with accounts of God's people sacrificing animals, building altars, making commitments to God, bringing offerings—long before God begins pouring out miracles.

People sometimes ask me, "Why do you take offerings at church? Is it just to cover the bills?"

I answer, "No, we are not just doing it to cover the bills. We are doing it because God clearly teaches the principle of bringing an offering to show our commitment to Him." Giving is a vital part of experiencing God's best for your life. You will never become all that

God wants you to become unless you shift from being a taker to being a giver.

There are many people who claim to love God, but they never give or contribute to anyone else. They only want to receive. How can we expect God to develop us into all He wants for us unless we imitate Him and become givers?

> "That which is not daring is nothing."
>
> — KENNETH PATCHEN

Does this just mean giving financially? No. It means giving in every area of your life. You will never fully experience the full blessing God has for your marriage unless you learn to care for your spouse. You will never reach the maximum potential of your small group or ministry unless you show up and say, "What can I give?" not, "What can I get?"

This is true for every aspect of life. Do you truly want to climb the ladder in your corporation or organization? Then, don't show up and say, "What am I going to get from them today?" Instead, ask, "How can I make this organization better?" You will begin to climb the ladder of success when you start focusing on being a giver rather than a taker. It could be said that giving is the rent you pay for being on this earth. You should leave it better than it was when you got here.

It is very important that we learn this principle of giving. Gideon made that commitment, and it made all the difference in the world for him, his family, and the entire nation of Israel.

■ Background Influences

Finally, Gideon had to deal with his past before he could move forward. Gideon came from a "weak" family, a family caught up in idolatry. He wasn't royalty. He wasn't of noble birth. His family was the least significant in his entire tribe. Gideon could have kept using that as an excuse for not obeying God's command, but he didn't.

All of us must deal with our pasts before we can become truly successful in unleashing our God-given dreams. Before you can move boldly into the future and discover God's best for your life, you must realize several basic "facts" about your past. Let me list a few of the more obvious:

YOU CAN'T CHANGE YOUR PAST

God can restore what Satan has tried to steal, and you may alter your perception of past events, but you cannot change what has already happened. The more you try, the more destructive you become to yourself. Your present situation is the result of all the choices you have made in the past, and it's true that others have made choices for you over which you had no control. However, that doesn't mean you can say that you're not responsible for your problems because they are the result of what someone else did.

"It's a funny thing about life; if you refuse to accept anything but the best, you very often get it."

— W. SOMERSET MAUGHAM

YOU CAN'T BLAME YOUR PAST

Some people are born with "silver spoons" in their mouths; others are deserted by their parents at birth. You have no control over what happened at birth, but your entire life will undoubtedly be touched forever by what happened during your first days and months. In the same way, you have no control over the past events of your life. You might have had a happy, nurturing family, or perhaps you grew up in an abusive home. Maybe your adult life has been good, or maybe you have been victimized by others. No matter what has happened in your past—especially those things over which you had no control—Christ is able to change you and work in you right now and in the future.

YOU DON'T NEED TO BE CONTROLLED BY YOUR PAST

Rearview mirrors are much smaller than windshields. We need to be much more focused on the road ahead—the future—than on what's behind us. Though past experiences and bad choices can be highly influential, you do not have to remain limited by them. If you are to succeed, you must come to terms with the events and people that have shaped your life, but you must refuse to use the past as a crutch or barrier any longer. There is a better way, as Gideon discovered.

■ Looking Back–Looking Forward

The better you understand how the past continues to influence how you think and act, the better equipped you will be to achieve great things, regardless of what happened in your past. Using the past as a foundation for the future isn't always easy, but it is possible.

Here are four suggestions that you can use to begin overcoming past influences:

TAKE RESPONSIBILITY FOR WHAT YOU HAVE BEEN, WHAT YOU ARE, AND WHAT YOU WILL BECOME

Don't spend your life blaming others for what has happened to you. And don't blame God. Simply take responsibility. Choose to live by the transformed and renewed mind God desires to give to you.

ASK GOD TO REVEAL HIS WILL, DREAMS AND GOALS TO YOU

People—even your loved ones—can be adept at placing their own restrictions on you. Traditions can imprison you. Because you can never live up to others' expectations, you may underachieve and feel rotten about yourself. Or, even worse, you may consistently perform below your capabilities because you let others determine what you're capable of doing.

DON'T AVOID CHANGE

Abraham Lincoln said, "You can't escape the responsibility of tomorrow by evading it today." Life's true winners get things sorted out, make the needed changes, and then concentrate on their own God-given dreams. Change can be frightening, but if you're going to experience God's best for your life, change you must.

BECOME A GIVER

What does God want you to bring to the altar to seal your commitment? Begin to give sacrificially today—give yourself, your time, your money, your talents—and watch what God can do in your life. Don't focus on the seed; focus on the harvest. The purpose of any seed is to create a harvest. Once you plant the seed, as Gideon did by bringing his offering to the altar, begin to expect the harvest that God desires to provide in your life. If you fail to expect your seed to produce, you rob it of the ability to do so. You must have expectation in the equation.

Leaving the past behind is not a passive activity. Often it hurts, since people sometimes misunderstand your motives. Yet truly successful people learn to leave the past behind, to live each day to the fullest, and to build toward the future. They learn to impact others positively, rather than allowing themselves to be influenced negatively. There is a cost, and it begins at an altar. That is one of the greatest steps you will make as you learn to seek God's best.

ACTION PLAN

First, spend some time in prayer. Tell God that you're willing to pay the price to follow Him. Then open up your notebook and write down some answers to the following questions:

1. Based on what you've read and learned so far, what do you believe is God's will for your life? (In other words, reiterate where you want to be five years from now and what you want to be doing.)

2. List some excuses you have been using to avoid following God's leading.

3. Write down experiences from your past that have made you feel like you're weak and insignificant.

4. What can you give (talents, time, resources, money) to seal your commitment to following God? Write this in the form of a specific goal and deadline: "By [date] I will [action plan]."

Now, be sure to follow through with your plan. It's an essential step to experiencing change and discovering God's best for your life.

GIDEON replied, "If now I have found favor in your eyes, give me a sign that it is really you talking to me. Please do not go away until I come back and bring my offering and set it before you." And the LORD said, "I will wait until you return." Gideon went in, prepared a young goat, and from an ephah of flour he made bread without yeast. Putting the meat in a basket and its broth in a pot, he brought them out and offered them to him under the oak.

(JUDGES 6:17–19)

STEP FOUR

ADOPT A NEW ATTITUDE

Gideon was a giver. But there is more to the story of the offering that Gideon gave than just meat and bread. Gideon wanted a sign. If the angel just ate the food, it undoubtedly would mean that the angel was only a man. If, on the other hand, the food was accepted as a sacrifice, it would mean much, much more.

The angel told Gideon to place the meat, cakes, and broth on a rock and then gave him an unmistakable sign:

> The angel of GOD stretched out the tip of the stick he was holding and touched the meat and the bread. Fire broke out of the rock and burned up the meat and bread while the angel of God slipped away out of sight. And Gideon knew it was the angel of God! Gideon said, "Oh no! Master, GOD! I have seen the angel of God face-to-face!" But GOD reassured him, "Easy now. Don't panic. You won't die." Then Gideon built an altar there to GOD and named it "GOD's Peace." It's still called that at Ophrah of Abiezer. (Judges 6:21–24, MSG)

Everything had changed. The commission Gideon had been given was not human in origin. It was divine. Gideon knew it and acknowledged it by immediately building an altar where his offering had been turned into a sacrifice.

But the story is far from over. In fact, this was just the beginning.

Breaking Down False Idols and Altars

For Gideon, the cost of answering God's call just got bigger. As the faithful through the centuries can testify, committing to God and becoming a giver are just the beginning of a new walk. So it was with Gideon:

> That same night the LORD said to him, "Take the second bull from your father's herd, the one seven years old. Tear down your father's altar to Baal and cut down the Asherah pole beside it. Then build a proper kind of altar to the LORD your God on the top of this height. Using the wood of the Asherah pole that you cut down, offer the second bull as a burnt offering." (Judges 6:25–26)

I am told that there are 331 times throughout Scripture where God says, as in Isaiah 1:19, "If you are willing and obedient, you will eat the best from the land."

"One person with courage makes a majority."

— ANDREW JACKSON

Steps that lead to commitment require faith. Steps that lead from the altar of commitment require not only faith but also obedience and much more. If you want to experience nothing less than God's best, much will be required from you. You must begin by allowing God to forge a new attitude in you as He leads you to discard many past hindrances to your obedience.

Gideon took ten of his servants and did as the Lord told him. "But because he was afraid of his family and the men of the town he did it at night rather than in the daytime" (Judges 6:27). It is easy to be judgmental here. Gideon was afraid, and he carried out God's instructions when no one was looking. We might look at Gideon's actions and wonder how he could ever defeat the Midianites if he couldn't even face his own family and neighbors. But keep in mind that, despite his fears, Gideon was obedient. That is more than can be said for so many people who say they want to do God's will.

Don't think that when you follow God your fears will vanish. Many times even when you are very afraid, faith calls you to move forward. Thankfully, we don't have to be ruled by fear. God's voice can overrule fear. That's why it is necessary to have the objective truth of God's Word.

The Bible is truth, and that is why you have to adjust your life to God's voice instead of expecting God to adjust to your whims and emotions. We run into all sorts of problems when we do that. Gideon was frightened, but when he knew what God wanted him to do, he trusted God's Word, stepped out in faith, and obeyed.

Keep in mind, however, that following God and doing what He tells you does not mean that your problems are all in the past. In fact, when Gideon did what God told him to do, everything seemed to go to pieces:

> "It is not good for all your wishes to be fulfilled. Through sickness you recognize the value of health; through evil the value of good; through hunger, satisfaction; through exertion, the value of rest."
>
> — HERACLITUS

In the morning when the men of the town got up, there was Baal's altar, demolished, with the Asherah pole beside it cut down and the second bull sacrificed on the newly built altar! They asked each other, "Who did this?" When they carefully investigated, they were told, "Gideon son of Joash did it." (Judges 6:28–29)

Notice that the men said that the son of Joash did it. Many Bible scholars believe that Gideon's father, Joash, one of the chief men of the city, was also one of the ringleaders of the idol worship. What the men were saying, then, was, "The guy who tore it down is the son of the guy who built it."

> Gideon became more known by his deeds than his creeds.

As often happens, Gideon, in his obedience to God's charge, had to begin forging a new direction by making changes close to home. Talk about messing up the family's heritage. Gideon tore down what his father had built. Furthermore, he offered a bull to God on the site where he tore down Baal's altar and the Asherah pole. The town fathers were not happy:

> The men of the town demanded of Joash, "Bring out your son. He must die, because he has broken down Baal's altar and cut down the Asherah pole beside it." But Joash replied to the hostile crowd around him, "Are you going to plead Baal's cause? Are you trying to save him? Whoever fights for him shall be put to death by morning. If Baal really is a god, he can defend himself when someone breaks down his altar." So that day they called Gideon "Jarub Baal," saying, "Let Baal contend with him," because he broke down Baal's altar. (Judges 6:30–32)

We as Christians always want to be known by what we believe. We like to talk about what we believe, but God is looking for doers of His Word. Knowing what you believe is important, but doing what you believe takes your life to the next level, and it requires an entirely new attitude.

Let me let you in on a little secret—most people don't care what you say or believe. That won't change anything for them. However,

what they see you do can make all the difference in the world, because your actions
follow your attitude. People don't care about
this verse or that creed. They believe what
they see. When they see a change in you,
then they'll be ready to listen to what you
say.

What are your deeds, not your creeds?
What are you doing that is different? Gideon
was not known because he said, "I saw God
and He talked to me, and I'm going to lead
you into war against the Midianites."

The people of the region would have undoubtedly said, "Yeah, Gideon. You talked
with God. Whatever! Just get out of the way
and let us get on with doing what we did
before you went totally weird."

> "If a grizzly was snapping at your heels, climbing a tree would seem like a small risk, wouldn't it? If you sit still, if you don't take risks, you're feeding the grizzly, not escaping it."
>
> — ROGER SMITH, FORMER CHAIRMAN OF GENERAL MOTORS

But something happened when Gideon talked with God. Everyone
knew it by the changes he made. They woke up in the morning and
the very idol the town was built around was torn down.

In short order, Gideon had to stand trial. To his credit, Gideon's
father, Joash, defended him. We aren't told why Joash went from being
a leader of Baal worship to standing up for his son. Maybe defending
his son was the natural thing for a parent to do; maybe there was
something more. Perhaps Gideon had explained to Joash during the
early-morning hours what he had done and why. We don't know.

All we know is that the attitude adjustment that began at the winepress and continued to the altar apparently spread from Gideon to his
father. What happened was amazing:

> But Joash replied to the hostile crowd around him, "Are you
> going to plead Baal's cause? Are you trying to save him? Who-
> ever fights for him shall be put to death by morning! If Baal

really is a god, he can defend himself when someone breaks down his altar." So that day they called Gideon "Jerub-Baal," saying, "Let Baal contend with him," because he broke down Baal's altar. (Judges 6:31–32)

Quickly, with a well-turned phrase—"if Baal is really a powerful god, then he can defend himself"—Gideon was not only delivered from the crowd's death threats but was given a new name as well. This name, Jerub-Baal (meaning "let Baal contend"), was a standing defiance of Baal and those who worshipped him. Given by Joash in the midst of a life-or-death standoff, it was a name that showed great honor to Gideon and the men who would follow him.

False Gods

What does this have to do with us today?

Let me explain Baal worship. Baal was a fertility god. It was a religion that involved crude sexual behavior. You name it and they did it in the name of Baal. There were all kinds of horrible, pornographic, sexually deviant activities involved in the worship of Baal. In fact, they had what was called an Asherah pole that was set up beside Baal. Temple prostitutes would gather and dance at this pole. (Yes, they had pole dancing even back then.) Then men would come and bring sacrifices to Baal, and lay them at the feet of the temple prostitutes. Does this sound a lot like modern-day strip clubs?

We think we are much more sophisticated than the Baal worshippers of Gideon's day. Sadly, there are people all around you and me who spend much more than 10 percent of their income on pornography and erotica. Maybe we aren't so sophisticated after all.

The people of Israel had embraced a religious system that gave, them an excuse to sin. They could lust and do whatever they wanted, all in the name of worship. Before they could be transformed into a nation that God could bless, Gideon had to confront his own sinful practices and those of his people.

He had to face his fears. God had spoken to him, so he had to go against many of the long-held standards that had left Israel so vulnerable to its enemies. Confronting people and sinful practices is never fun, but when you do, life can get exciting very quickly. As you ask God to purify you, He can begin to do great things through you.

"To dare is to lose one's footing momentarily. To not dare is to lose oneself."

— SOREN KIERKENGAARD

Granted, you probably don't worship Baal or go to an Asherah pole. But are there any false "gods" in your life?

FALSE IDOLS

Clearly the Asherah pole and Baal worship are idols. Idolatry represents wrong allegiances and misguided devotion—really, anything that takes the place of God. Sometimes we have to face our wrong priorities or maybe someone else's, as Gideon had to do for himself and his father. Facing false gods and wrong priorities will lead you to examine everything from how much money you spend to how much time you give to things that in the end really do not matter in life.

FAMILY SINS

Gideon had to tear down the Asherah pole that his father had built. We learn a lot of our false worship from our parents and our culture. Maybe you learned destructive habits or attitudes from a spouse, a brother, a sister, a parent, or a roommate, and as a result you began to settle for less than God's best. Understand that when you decide to change, people—even your loved ones—may get upset with you.

Did you know that 87 percent of the people in America never break out of the social class they were born into? Why? They've never learned that they actually could break out. They've been told, "You were born into this situation and you've got to stay here."

A friend of mine was the first in his family to go to college. When he went, rather than congratulating him, his family became angry. Thankfully, he stuck with his new goals and by his actions began to set a new standard for all the children in his family to follow.

Someone has to face the sins and false worship that have settled into a family or culture for generation after generation. Someone like Gideon finally has to say, "That's it. From this point, we're going to do things differently. We are going to follow God. We are going to have an attitude adjustment that will make a difference for generations to come."

SEXUAL IMMORALITY

Gideon, for all we know, was a participant in the sexual immorality of Baal worship that permeated the region where he grew up. At the very least, he would have been exposed to it and influenced by it. Therefore, he had to face his own sexual immorality. He also had to face his father's immorality and the whole city's sexual sins. He had to stand up against the filth all around him.

> "Strength has a million faces."
>
> — DES'REE

A man recently came to me with a similar problem. Every year he went with a group of friends and coworkers to a big sales convention in another part of the country. He said to me, "Since I'm following God now, I just don't feel comfortable going. There are a lot of things that go on there that I really don't want to be involved with anymore. I have to go to the convention because it's part of my job, so what I really need is the guts to stand up and say, 'I'm not going to join in on the other activities.' Would you pray with me, pastor?"

I said, "Absolutely."

We prayed right there.

When he arrived at the convention, he refused to join in the questionable activities. At first, his coworkers were angry with him because his stand for righteousness highlighted their own immorality. But eventually the salesman's actions caused the entire group to rethink what they had been doing. Each person in the group had secretly been praying that someone would have the courage to do the right thing. That man's decision made it easier for all of them to stop doing things that could cause such guilt and damage to their marriages and families. One man's courageous stand changed everything.

PEER PRESSURE

Do you think Gideon faced peer pressure? The townsfolk were going to kill him. He messed up their system. A lot of times we think that teens are the only ones who deal with peer pressure. Adults face it too. That's why we drive expensive cars and live in houses that we can't afford. Why? Because all of our friends have them, so we think we should too.

> "Leadership is action, not position."
>
> — DONALD MCGANNON

It never dawns on us that we should have what we can afford, not what we can't afford. We feel peer pressure to live at a certain level. Peer pressure in itself isn't a sin. But giving in to it—regardless of your age—can be crippling and destructive to you and your family.

INTIMIDATION

Gideon was intimidated by his father and all the other men in town. Likewise, the intimidation of other people often keeps us from attempting to fulfill the dreams that God has given us. We may have a clear dream, but then we think, "What would my mother/father/sister/brother/friend say about that?"

Many times we are intimidated by someone who is very vocal. He or she may have an abrasive personality. You think, "I don't

"Failure can be bought on easy terms; success must be paid for in advance."

— CULLEN HIGHTOWER

want to face them." If we always ask the question, "What would so-and-so think?" we will never attempt anything.

Here is a good alternative question: "What does God think? What does God think about my allowing this person to hold me back from the dreams that God has given me?" You might as well call the person who intimidates you a "god," because he or she is determining your life steps. But if the Lord is truly God, then you have to go where God is leading you, even if the most abrasive personalities in the room don't agree. You have to obey anyway.

If God has placed something on your heart and you are gifted for it and it does not go against Scripture, then go for it. As long as your dreams and goals line up with God's Word, follow them, even if a "false voice" doesn't understand, gets angry, or tries to intimidate you into going another direction.

NEGATIVE IMAGES

Did you grow up with a good image of yourself? People often grow up in negative environments. That's a proven fact. Dr. Shad Helmstetter, a leading psychologist and best-selling author of *What to Say When You Talk to Yourself*, has developed research that is shocking:

> During the first eighteen years of our lives, if we grew up in fairly average, reasonably positive homes, we were told 'No!,' or what we could not do, more than 148,000 times. . . . Meanwhile, during the same period, the first eighteen years of your life, how often do you suppose you were told what you can do or what you can accomplish in life? A few thousand times? A few hundred? During my speaking engagements to groups

across the country, I have had people tell me they could not remember being told what they could accomplish in life more than three or four times! Whatever the number, for most of us, the yeses we received simply didn't balance out the noes.

Dr. Helmstetter relates the fact that prominent psychologists, psychiatrists and researchers in the behavioral sciences almost universally agree that as much as 77 percent of everything we think is detrimental and negative. Coincidentally, researchers in the medical field say that as much as 75 percent of all diseases and disorders are self-induced.

That means that as much as 75 percent or more of our programming is the harmful, negative kind. Year after year our thoughts have been influenced. We have, in effect, become our own worst enemies. There has to be a better way.

When we face our fears and dethrone our false idols, the results are always worth it. Sometimes the only thing that will give us the emotional fortitude to face our fears is the knowledge that results will indeed come. Time and again when you see God do a great

> "The common idea that success spoils people by making them vain, egotistic, and self-complacent is erroneous; on the contrary, it makes them, for the most part, humble, tolerant, and kind. Failure makes people cruel and bitter."
>
> — W. SOMERSET MAUGHAM

work with someone, they have to face their fears and step out on faith. But when they do that, when they follow God's leading, look what happens. After Gideon had passed the test by facing down the idolatry of his family and town, "Then the spirit of the LORD came upon Gideon" (Judges 6:34). Then came the power! Obedience brings power. A new attitude causes strength and direction to flow into your life.

"Relentless, repetitive
self-talk is what
changes our
self-image."

— DENIS WAITLEY

We often wonder why some people have power in their lives and are more successful than others. They are successful because they have passed tests, small and large, that you have not passed yet. There are only eleven times in all of Scripture that specifically say that the Spirit of the Lord came upon someone. God's power comes when tests are passed.

Are you passing the test that God has put in front of you? Is there a fear you need to face? Is there a person or a problem you need to face? Are there "false gods" you need to break down?

On the other side of the tests—as you forge a new attitude—is a life where you will experience the best that God has for you.

Questioning God

Just as your blood must continually be recycled from the heart to the lungs to the outer reaches of your body and back again to maintain life, your attitude must also be recycled through these facets of your soul and spirit. It must constantly be transformed by the renewing of your mind. You must constantly seek to understand what God wants you to become. In short, your goal should be to always raise your level of strategic thinking to God's level.

What I'm trying to say is that we need to learn to trust God, even when we don't understand everything about what He is asking us to do. If you say, "I'll follow God when I understand exactly why everything happens," then you never will. Don't waste your life asking the wrong questions. Spend your life on the right questions, doing the right things.

What are the right questions?

Questions such as, "God, how can I be used by You? How can I fit into Your purpose? How can I give myself to You more completely?" God will answer those questions far beyond anything you can imagine.

But instead we often ask, "Why don't things ever work out for me? Why haven't I seen miracles in my life like so-and-so? Why me?" Those questions scream out our lack of trust and dependence upon Him.

> You cannot perform in a way that is inconsistent with how you feel about yourself.

God blesses His work. Instead of Him getting into your business, He is asking you to join Him in His. There's a difference. We have to discover what He wants for us and the direction He is leading us to go. We have to raise our thinking to God's way of thinking in order to raise our life to the abundant life He has for us.

God asked Gideon to change the way he thought. Gideon had to break down an altar to a false god and destroy a way of thinking that had literally opened his family and nation to their enemies. To do that, Gideon had to stop thinking of himself as weak and insignificant.

You cannot perform in a way that is inconsistent with how you feel about yourself. If you think you're a loser, you will take the action steps that losers take. In order to experience God's best, you need to stop thinking that you cannot do anything, that you have no strength, and that you have no power.

You have incredible gifts.

Begin to realize that you have gifts, talents, abilities, and dreams, and that God equipped you for such a time as this. When you begin to think this way, it is amazing how you will act.

In other words, the number one thing you have to change is not your circumstances, environment, relationships, family, or income. The number one thing that you must change is the way you think. Changing your attitude will change your altitude—how high you go in life. That one simple thing will bring an amazing transformation into your life.

You will not experience God's best in your life and your marriage until you begin to change your attitude toward your spouse. You are not going to grow in your career unless you change your attitude

> "Don't go after money. Go after success. If you have the success, they'll throw the money at you."
>
> — ED MCMAHON

toward your boss and those with whom you work. You are not going to be able to expect more from God in your personal walk with Him unless you change your attitude toward God and His Word. You are not going to be able to see more happen with your kids until you change your parenting attitude toward them.

When you change your attitude toward your problems, then the problem is more likely to change. Until your attitude changes, nothing else will. Let me show you why.

The Creative Process

If your attitude doesn't change, then the creative process cannot flow within you. This creativity, once you are open to it, will give you new answers to old problems. However, if you have the same attitude, you won't even attempt to change.

I often hear people say, "Well, you know my husband (or wife). He (or she) is never going to change." If you truly believe that, you will never do anything different, since you don't believe that person will ever change. What's the use of trying?

You don't have a resource problem; you have an idea problem. You don't have a marriage problem; you have an idea problem. You don't have a career problem; you have an idea problem. Until your attitude changes, you won't open yourself to new ideas for those problems. You won't even be able to come up with a good, workable plan for change.

You will never excel beyond your attitude. A sour attitude equals a sour life. A great attitude equals a great life.

Does that mean that you won't have trials and tribulations when you begin developing a new attitude? No. In fact there is no one in the world who doesn't currently have problems. Everyone faces difficult circumstances. We often think we would have a better attitude if we didn't have all these problems, but the only place we will never have problems is in heaven.

The truth is that when you finally do become successful, you just get a new set of problems. To be alive is to have problems. Without problems you cannot become a conqueror. So your attitude really does determine your altitude.

"We are called to become creators, to make the world new."

— JOHN BOODIN

Motivation guru Dan Lier, a salesman at the time, went to talk with another very successful salesman to learn from him. At that time, Dan was in his thirties. The other salesman was twenty-four years old and only three years into his career, straight out of college. The young man was already earning $250,000 a year. This guy was on fire, blowing past everyone's quotas and expectations. Dan wanted to learn what made the young salesman so different. So when they got together, Dan took out his notebook and pen and began asking questions.

They had not talked long before the younger salesman interrupted Dan and said, "I've got to tell you something that will change your life." Dan got ready to write the magical words.

"You will never make $250,000 a year."

Dan sat there stunned, appalled by the young man's lack of confidence in him.

"Please hear me out," the young salesman continued. "I like you. I think you're a nice guy. I don't know you well, and I don't know your family. I don't even know your business or exactly how you sell. But I can tell you this, Dan. You will never earn a quarter-million a year with a hundred-grand attitude."

Dan was taken aback, but it soon became crystal clear that the younger man was telling the truth. He had gotten comfortable making $100,000. His mind wouldn't even allow him to think realistically about making $250,000.

> "Choosing to be positive and having a grateful attitude is going to determine how you're going to live your life."
>
> — JOEL OSTEEN

The point is simple. If your attitude doesn't change—if you can't conceive it—you can't achieve it. If you don't think you can ever cross a chasm, you will never try to build a bridge.

This is true no matter where you are right now. If you're earning $20,000 a year and you dream of earning $40,000 a year, unless your attitude goes there first you will never earn it.

If you are the pastor of a church running one hundred and you dream of pastoring the next Lakewood Church in Houston, unless your attitude goes through the same process that Joel Osteen's did, you will never have thirty-five thousand members.

You have to break out of the mind-set that continues to hold you back. Husbands and wives, you have to develop a new attitude toward your spouse before your marriage can get better. Parents, you have to break out of the old mind-set of the past before you can see true change happening in your children. If you're a business owner, you have to expand your mind and get an entirely new way of thinking, talking, and acting before you can build the huge, successful business that you desire.

A new way of life has a price tag. Success will never happen unless it happens first in your heart and mind. That is why a new attitude will change everything for you.

Practical Steps toward a New Attitude

One of the most startling discoveries of life takes place when you realize that you have the power to choose what kind of day you are going to have. Each day comes to you neutral. It is neither up nor down. You choose whether you will be positive or negative.

The mood of your day is not set by circumstances, by other people, by tasks you have to do, by events that happen along the way. It is set by one thing—your attitude. You may not always be able to control what happens in the course of a day, but you can always control the way you react to what happens.

Let me suggest six very practical steps. Though these steps are not directly from Judges 6 or 7, I can tell you that these everyday hints can help you develop a new attitude.

BEFORE YOU GO TO BED AT NIGHT, PREPARE FOR THE NEXT DAY

Even though you might be tired, spend a little time each night reflecting on the good things that have happened that day. Lay out your clothes. Make or check to-do lists for the next day. John D. Rockefeller said that the last thing he did before he went to bed every night was to empty his pockets very slowly. As he took each object out of his pocket, he made a conscious effort to empty his mind of all worry, anxiety, and negative thoughts.

DECIDE TO START EVERY DAY WITH A GREAT ATTITUDE

The most important hour in each day is not "happy hour"—it is the first hour you are awake. That first hour sets the pace for the remainder of the day. Starting out the day on a positive note sets a tone for positive thoughts all day, which is the emotional version of the law of inertia.

KEEP YOUR OBJECTIVES CLEAR

Suffice it to say that your goals are only as good as the way they are focused in your mind. Visualize yourself reaching your goals and replay that mental picture as often as you can. Then, no matter what arises, you will be able to keep your sense of direction.

KEEP REMINDING YOURSELF WHY YOU WANT TO SUCCEED

One businessman has been asked many times why he succeeded when people he grew up with never made it. His simple answer is: "I guess I just had more reasons to get rich than they did." One of the best ways to keep yourself motivated is to focus on as many good reasons to succeed as you can think of. Then, keep reminding yourself of all those reasons. You can accomplish the most incredible things if you have enough reasons to.

SEE YOURSELF AS AN ACHIEVER, NOT A TRY-ER

The world is filled with people who merely give life one halfhearted shot after another and then wonder why they never succeed. No one wins every time, but you can plan to achieve the highest goals in everything you do. Keep reminding yourself that you don't have to run second to anybody. To life's champions, it is never enough to simply be glad to be in the game; they are always in it to win it.

REMEMBER THAT ACHIEVEMENT INVITES CRITICISM

Criticism has been around for a long time, and our society has honed it to a razor-sharp edge. Here's how the *Chicago Times* in 1865 evaluated Abraham Lincoln's Gettysburg Address: "The cheek of every American must tingle with shame as he reads the silly, flat, and dish-watery utterances of a man who has to be pointed out to intelligent foreigners as President of the United States."

When Henry Ward Beecher was preaching in Brooklyn, he carried a handful of flowers into the pulpit one Sunday and placed them in a vase that they might adorn the stand from which he spoke. The next day, the New York newspapers carried lengthy articles condemning Beecher for "desecrating the pulpit with flowers!"

Samuel Morse attempted to get money from Congress for a telegraph line from Baltimore to Washington, and he had to endure the adverse criticisms of the press for eleven years.

A six-year-old lad came home with a note from his teacher in which it was suggested that he be taken out of school, as he was "too stupid to learn." That boy was Thomas Edison.

When Adam Thompson built the first bathtub in America in 1845, the newspapers said he was "going to spoil the democratic simplicity of the republic."

When Cyrus Field was trying to lay the Atlantic cable, newspapers denounced his cable as "a mad freak of stubborn ignorance."

A New York evening paper dated Saturday, May 21, 1927, contained an inside page that featured an elaborate demonstration by some expert giving overwhelming proof that Charles Lindbergh could not make his New York-to-Paris flight. Ironically, the front page of that same paper, hastily typeset just before going to print, proclaimed in huge headline type the news that Lindbergh had arrived safely in France.

> "Success is to be measured not so much by the position that one has reached in life as by the obstacles which he has overcome while trying to succeed."
>
> — BOOKER T. WASHINGTON

In 1929 Sam Goldwyn was looking for an actress to play opposite Ronald Coleman in *Raffles*. At his casting director's suggestion, he ran a screen test of an unknown actress. After viewing the test, Goldwyn jumped out of his chair shouting, "What are you guys trying to do to me? You think I'm going to hire a dame with those big pop-eyes who talks funny like she does?" Several years later, Sam Goldwyn gladly paid top-dollar for the same young woman to star in such MGM hit movies as *The Little Foxes*. The actress? Sultry-eyed Bette Davis.

When Englishman David Puttnam offered his latest screenplay to Columbia Pictures, the reply he received stated, "I'm sorry to tell you this has no validity at all in the American marketplace, because of the style and tone as well as the subject matter." That motion picture, *Chariots of Fire*, won the 1981 Oscar for best picture.

It simply is not realistic to think that you can achieve anything in life without experiencing the barbs of criticism and disappointment.

However, when those stinging comments come, remind yourself that you are in excellent company.

▬ Keep Yourself Up

No one is the best at everything all the time. By definition, you cannot succeed unless you encounter challenges. Sometimes you will fail, perhaps miserably. But when you fail, don't ask, "Will I keep getting knocked down?" but, "Will I keep getting up?"

The record books are filled with stories about people who failed time and again but ultimately succeeded:

- Babe Ruth held the record for strikeouts long before he set the home-run record. The Babe once said, "I may have my faults, but givin' up ain't one of 'em."

- Henry Ford forgot to include a reverse gear in his first car. Later, the Father of Mass Production said, "I always learn more from my failures than from my successes."

- Thomas Edison tried thousands of materials before he found the one that made his incandescent light work. He said, "The three great essentials to achieve anything worthwhile are, first, hard work; second, stick-to-it-iveness; third, common sense."

- Cy Young, for whom professional baseball's most coveted award for pitcher of the year is named, was a great star, yet he only won 511 big league games out of the 906 that he pitched—just slightly more than half.

Successful people in the past often had mediocre talents and questionable skills. Most struggled against overwhelming odds. All had many reasons to give up. But they kept going, despite the losses, until they overcame the odds.

Gideon was the runt of the family, hidden away in a winepress, cowering from the Midianites. Yet, when he heard the voice of God, something changed. He got an entirely new attitude, one that immediately affected those around him and eventually changed the course of history.

Will you find a way to develop a new attitude? Can you simply refuse to stay down? Can you focus on results, not on problems? Will you be able to keep yourself motivated?

To be an outstanding success in any endeavor, it is not necessary to be right all the time. If you are right more than half the time, you may win a gold medal, make a million dollars, invent a new computer component, develop a cure for a dreaded disease, pastor the world's largest church, or join the top level of your industry. You can also improve your marriage, become a better parent, start a new ministry, or just live a more satisfying and fulfilling life.

> "Normal is not something to aspire to; it's something to get away from."
>
> – JODIE FOSTER

The idea is to keep doing the things that successful people do. And successful people always point to an achieving attitude as their top priority.

■ Looking Back–Looking Forward

My father and mother are two of my greatest heroes. Both had plenty of reasons to have the worst attitude in the world. Instead they decided at critical points in their lives not to be held back by the past. They created a legacy of winning and achievement that has permeated my life.

My dad, Bill Cornelius, was born in Blythe, California, in the middle of nowhere. His parents were migrant farmworkers. He lived in a car as his parents drove from town to town, getting work wherever they could. My dad went to eleven different elementary schools before he reached the fifth grade. Somehow, he eventually finished high school and entered the Air Force. When he got out of the service, Dad decided to use Uncle Sam's GI Bill offer and go to college. After he graduated, he taught school for a while and then was employed by NASA, where he worked on all the Apollo missions. Later, he worked for decades with a major corporation in Houston. Along the way, he developed a number of rental and investment properties. He and my mother have been financially independent for years.

My mom grew up in San Antonio. She became a Christian when she was in high school, but her father was dead set against her following God. He was rebellious toward God and abusive toward his family, but my mother literally prayed him into heaven. My grandfather finally received Christ into his heart on his deathbed. She prayed for my father too, and not long after he left NASA for the corporate world, he accepted the Lord.

Due to my mother, our family now has a heritage of faith. Everything I do as the pastor of a large church is mostly due to what I learned by watching them.

My dad is not a celebrity (except to me!). He has never preached a sermon. Yet he is a godly man who loves the Lord and supports the work of God through his local church, worldwide missions, and other ministries. His faithfulness is an inspiration to anyone who knows him.

My mom held neighborhood Bible clubs and stayed active in the local church. Children who came to the Lord through her backyard ministry are scattered around the world now, ministering Jesus Christ, because she was so faithful.

I know what a new attitude, not limited by the past, can do for a family and a community. I have lived with parents who epitomized what God wants to do in every person.

Like Gideon, they learned firsthand that great achievement comes from the deep, inner conviction that you can succeed in whatever you do, regardless of yesterday's failures or today's odds.

How about you?

You, and you alone, can control who you are from the inside out. Once you have heard the voice of God, nothing less than His best will be satisfying. When you decide to become all that the Lord desires for you to be, nothing can hold you back.

ACTION PLAN

First, spend some time in prayer and talk to God about your current attitude. Ask him to help you change the way you think about your life and current circumstances. Then take out your notebook and write down your answers to the following questions:

1. What do you do best?

2. What do you do poorly?

3. What would you like to stop doing?

4. What would you like to start doing?

5. What would you like to change most about your attitude—the way you face life every day?

6. Write down three specific things you will do to change your attitude this week.

GIDEON said to God,

"If you will save Israel by my hand as you have promised—look, I will place a wool fleece on the threshing floor. If there is dew only on the fleece and all the ground is dry, then I will know that you will save Israel by my hand, as you said." And that is what happened. Gideon rose early the next day; he squeezed the fleece and wrung out the dew—a bowlful of water. Then Gideon said to God, "Do not be angry with me. Let me make just one more request. Allow me one more test with the fleece. This time make the fleece dry and the ground covered with dew." That night God did so. Only the fleece was dry; all the ground was covered with dew.

(JUDGES 6:36–40)

STEP FIVE

DEVELOP A PLAN

Nearly every Sunday school student has heard the story of Gideon's fleece. I remember seeing it portrayed on the flannel board with a big puffy piece of cotton playing the part of the fleece. I have also heard plenty of sermons since then about the fleece, many times with Gideon being chided for his lack of faith.

"The need for signs," I heard, "points to wavering faith. People who are mature in the Lord don't need signs."

What?

Gideon was anything but mature in the Lord. He had just met the angel of the Lord in the winepress. Life had become a blur as he prepared to go into battle against the greatest army of his generation.

Let's cut Gideon a little slack here. His trial by fire is coming soon. He is trying to sort things out and figure out what to do next. God wants to be believed, and Gideon wanted to believe Him.

And the fleece was an important step in that process.

▬ The Fleece

Gideon was struggling to put everything in perspective. He had responded to the angel's call. He had torn down the idol of Baal and the Asherah pole and committed himself to following God's leading. The

Spirit of God had come upon him. Bit by bit, he was being prepared to lead his army against the Midianites.

Now Gideon asks for a sign to confirm that God is with him. He lays out a fleece (sheepskin) and asks God to soak the fleece with dew the next morning and keep the surrounding ground dry.

It's important to note that God didn't condemn Gideon for asking for this sign. When the morning came, and Gideon found the fleece dewy and the ground dry, it raised the level of his faith.

Just to be sure, Gideon followed up with a second test. This time he asked that the fleece be dry and the ground wet.

Again, God didn't condemn him for his request. The next morning, the fleece was dry and the ground wet, just as Gideon had asked. As a result, his faith and expectation rose even higher.

The lesson is unmistakable. By granting Gideon's request, God showed how tender He is toward true believers. He wants us to believe Him. You see, the difference between people who discover change in their lives and those who don't is rarely about talent or skill. The difference is expectation, faith, trust.

That is why God gives holy experiences. The God we serve is a God of purpose. He brought you to where you are for a purpose, and He wants your faith to increase because of the experiences He gives.

Think of Mary, the mother of Jesus. The angel of the Lord announced to this young woman that she would bear God's Son, the Messiah, and then the Holy Spirit came upon her and she was with child. That experience raised her expectation, giving her faith for the challenges of explaining everything to Joseph and her parents. It also gave her the courage to stand strong in spite of the scorn and withering criticism that must have come from relatives and neighbors.

"To know is not to prove, nor to explain. It is to accede to vision. But if we are to have vision, we must learn to participate in the object of vision. The apprenticeship is hard."

— ANTOINE DE SAINT-EXUPÉRY

Consider Jesus' disciples. Jesus announced the birth of the church before he returned to heaven. After that came the outpouring of the Holy Spirit as recorded in Acts 2:1–4. Those in the Upper Room received power. The church was born. Everything changed, and the gates of hell have never been able to stamp out God's church, the movement that continues to spread worldwide.

Gideon used the fleece to make sure that it was God who was speaking to him. But even though the fleece was important, Gideon still wasn't ready to take on the task God was giving him.

Winning Your War First

So many times we want to skip ahead to Gideon's victory without observing the preparations he had to make. Everyone wants to watch the super-heavyweight champion of the world win the big fight. No one wants to watch him when he is shadowboxing in the middle of some dark, dusty, old gym. No one cheers him on for eight hours straight every single day as he readies himself for the fight. No one wants to watch that part, but that is where the fight is won.

The fleece was part of Gideon's preparation. God is about to lead Gideon into battle, but it took a process of getting ready.

At this point, God had clearly confirmed His will to Gideon in three different ways. First He spoke to him, and then He made the fleece dewy and the ground dry. Then He made the ground wet and the fleece dry. Gideon had three clear signs to move forward at this point.

Some might call it a lack of faith or preparation overkill. Call it whatever you want. What we do know is that during the time leading up to the battle against the Midianites, Gideon wasn't sitting back and relaxing. He was busily putting together a battle plan.

The fleece confirmed to Gideon that he was headed in the right direction. But he didn't assume that he had no further responsibility, that victory would be automatic. Instead, he was correctly answering the major questions that came to mind. Why? What? How? When? These were critical questions to ask.

Everyone I know wants God to bless them. The difference between those who seem "blessed" versus those who just talk big is simple: The ones who get blessed have a plan.

> "People seldom hit what they do not aim at."
>
> — HENRY DAVID THOREAU

Do you have a plan? When your dreams go from your head to a calendar and a to-do list, you have a plan. As we are about to see, Gideon got inspired, and then he put together a plan.

Then and now, inspiration without planning leads to frustration and failure. Inspiration that leads to perspiration ends with success. Gideon was finding this out.

It is time that we also learn the great lessons of developing solid ways to fulfill God's vision.

Your Vision—Your Plan

Putting together a specific nuts-and-bolts action plan is vital to your success as you learn to seek God's best.

Why?

A wise person once said, "Stumbling on pebbles doesn't hurt as much when you're climbing toward a mountain peak."

For example, I pastor Bay Area Fellowship. Since its inception, it has been one of the fastest-growing churches in America. Over the years, we have been involved in some pretty big building projects. Each time, it never ceases to amaze me how much time it takes to do all the substratum and foundation work.

Building a beautiful facility requires much more than sketching out a plan, joining a few beams together, stringing a few lights, and hiring an interior decorator. It is understandable that it would take time to prepare everything. However, sometimes it seems that the longest and largest amounts of expense and mental output take place in the architectural offices and muddy foundation trenches, long before people see a structure emerge above the ground.

Yet no one considers the planning and foundational work ridiculous or unreasonable. The architects, contractors, and project managers—if they are to stay in business—must take each step of preparation very seriously. Beyond that, no matter what stage the construction may be at, you can be guaranteed that a complete set of blueprints and a detailed timetable are always handy at the construction site.

Why, then, do people think they must rush headlong into the "action" without a complete set of plans? Sure, the plans may change. Yes, you will face challenges. But if you are to be successful, you must have a carefully constructed master plan that includes:

> Putting together a specific nuts-and-bolts action plan is vital to your success.

- Your WHY—overall reason, vision or concept

- Your WHAT—specific goals

- Your HOW—action strategies

- Your WHEN—timetable

Let me put it in an equation or formula:

Why + What + How + When = Your Successful Master Plan

Without this master plan, your "building" will be haphazard at best and dangerous at worst. A well-crafted, detailed master plan, on the other hand, will help propel you more certainly toward success so that you don't have to keep putting out "fleeces" at each step.

After all, before you set out on any journey, you ought to know something about where you want to go, what you want to do, how you are going to get there, and when you expect to arrive. Let's take the remainder of this chapter to look at your WHY, WHAT, HOW, and WHEN questions.

■ Your WHY

The necessary ingredient in any formula for success is vision—your underlying, driving, desire-filled WHY. This is why Solomon, considered one of history's wisest men, said: "Where there is no vision, the people perish" (Proverbs 29:18, KJV).

God gave Gideon an unmistakable vision: "Save Israel out of Midian's hand. Am I not sending you?" (Judges 6:14, KJV).

Maybe your vision won't come quite so dramatically, but it needs to be crystal clear. You need to have this vision to keep going when you are tired, misunderstood, weary, and want to quit. During those times, your WHY gives you the inspiration to keep going forward, even when everything—and everyone—else tells you otherwise.

Daniel Boone, the American frontiersman and trailblazer, once quipped, "I can't say I was ever lost, but I was bewildered once for three days." What he pointed to was the fact that many people are handicapped by shortsightedness. Focusing mainly on things right in front of you, rather than having a farsighted view, is one of the major causes of failure, or—to use Daniel Boone's word—being bewildered.

> It's better to shoot for the moon and hit the picket fence than to aim for the fence and hit the ground.

To be successful, you must somehow find a way to look past barriers and potential failures. Napoleon saw

Italy, not the Alps. George Washington saw victory over the Hessians at Trenton, not the frozen Delaware River. American miler Glenn Cunningham did not concentrate on his burned, scarred legs, but instead visualized himself as an Olympic medalist. Billy Graham followed his calling to take the Gospel around the world rather than seeing all the obstacles to worldwide evangelism.

Most men and women see the obstacles, but successful people are able to look past barriers and see the goal. How about you? What will it take to stop you? You will never be any more successful than your goals. You will have an opportunity to write out your vision—your WHY—at the end of this chapter.

Your WHAT

Everyone dreams and sets goals. How often have you heard people say, "I just never set goals," or, "I don't believe in goals—that way, I am never disappointed if I don't reach them." That may sound good, but it's not true.

Everyone sets goals every day. We either turn off the alarm or keep snoozing. We choose to eat breakfast or to skip that meal. Either we to go to work or we stay home and become couch potatoes. We choose either to pay the bills or let the electricity be switched off, either to run two miles or eat two candy bars. Whether you realize it or not, you are constantly making choices and setting goals. We have become so accustomed to setting and reaching those everyday goals that we don't even realize what we are doing.

> "Every experience God gives us, every person He puts in our lives, is the perfect preparation for the future that only He can see."
> — CORRIE TEN BOOM

The same thought applies to your daily, weekly, monthly, yearly, and lifetime goals. You are dreaming of doing *something*.

After years of studying and working with people from all walks of life, I can tell you that the one thing that sets successful people apart is that they are generally better dreamers and goal-setters. I can safely say that the overwhelming majority of truly successful people got that way by identifying their personal dreams and goals, and by following orderly paths to reach those levels.

Likewise, clearly defined and pursued goals give direction to your life. Your aspirations rise and fall on your goals. No plan can ever be any better than the goals on which it is founded.

In order to be effective, your goals must have certain characteristics.

PERSONAL

You must be able to be excited about your goals. They must be internally motivated, since external expectations quickly lose luster. If you are excited about your goals, you can use them to process everything else out and to focus all your energies and resources toward accomplishing them. On the contrary, if your goals do not excite you, neither will they motivate you to change.

FUTURE-ORIENTED

You should base your goals upon the future, not the past. Granted, the past can be a foundation. But when God decides to do the supernatural in your life, He often does a new thing.

Decide that your goal should have little or nothing to do with past accomplishments or past failures. Have you ever read the warning on mutual funds—"past performance does not necessarily guarantee future performance"? I would say the same thing with humans. Just because you failed last year doesn't mean that you will fail this year. In fact, failure shows that at least you tried. Thus, you have a much better shot at succeeding this year.

Look at national champions in almost every sport. In almost every case, they were beaten the year before. Yes, there are dynasties, but those dynasties always experience previous failure as they learn to get to the next level.

Failure means that you have discovered one more way not to get something done. Anything worth doing is worth doing poorly at first!

SPECIFIC

The more specific your goals, the better your chances of reaching each milepost. Time after time, I have observed that people who set specific goals see things happen, while people who don't set goals end up waiting for something to happen—and wishful thinkers sit around wondering what happened.

GOD-BASED

Don't base the goal upon who you are but *Whose* you are. You never base a goal upon what you think you are, but base it upon who God is. If Gideon had set his goals based upon who he was, he never would have faced the Midianites. It was his confidence in God that led him to lead his people against a far more powerful nation.

We often set our goals much too small and give ourselves such limited time to reach the goal. We overestimate what we can do in a small time, and we underestimate what we can do in a lifetime. When we set our goals with God in mind, there is no limit to what we can achieve.

ACHIEVABLE

A goal is not some vague pipe dream or pie-in-the-sky fantasy. A good goal is one that causes you to stretch all your abilities, yet one that you can be reasonably confident of attaining. Only you know the difference between a true goal and a fantasy.

Meaningful, achievable goals can be broken down into three basic categories: 1. *Long-range goals* cover several years, but usually not more than three to five years. 2. *Intermediate goals* are long-range goals broken down into six-month or one-year steps, always leading toward the long-range goals you have set. 3. *Short-range goals* come from breaking down your intermediate goals into monthly or weekly steps toward your long-range goals.

BALANCED

Your goals should cover every aspect of your life. Many people fail to reap the full benefit of goal setting because they confine their goals only to one area of their lives. I never cease to be amazed at how the most outstanding goal-setters among business and civic leaders are sometimes complete failures at setting goals with their families. Likewise, some college professors have marvelous intellectual goals, yet they completely ignore their need for physical-fitness goals. As you set your goals, don't forget that success hinges on how you keep them in balance in the various areas of your life.

> "Most people fail because they fail to understand what they are trying to do."
> — LOU HOLTZ

WRITTEN

You must write down your goals. This is critical. Just like making a grocery list or daily to-do list, recording your goals on paper externalizes them and helps you be more accountable for fulfilling them. Also, the act of writing down what you want to accomplish helps you think through the steps you'll need to take and gives you a guideline around which you can plan your daily, weekly, monthly, and yearly activities.

The value of setting and writing down goals to achieve your personal or professional dreams cannot be overemphasized. There is a certainty that comes with written goals. The difference between their being in your head and being written is that when they are on paper, your goals are much more certain in an uncertain world. Everything else can change, but with written goals, you always know where you are going!

Everything you do, especially as you set your goals, has a definite impact on where you are going to be five years from now.

■ Your HOW

It's not enough to have a vision and specific goals. You also must have a plan for accomplishing those goals. Your WHY vision statement forms the foundation for your WHAT goals, which then become the bedrock for your HOW action strategies.

A powerful action plan—your daily, weekly, and monthly steps, as well as next year's schedule—will help you attain your goals. In fact, no matter how strong your WHY, WHAT, and WHEN may be, they are useless without your HOW action strategies.

During World War I, German submarines were causing considerable concern for the Americans. Someone asked cowboy satirist Will Rogers, "What would you do about the subs if you were president?"

"That's easy," the humorist grinned. "I'd drain the Atlantic Ocean dry, and then you could see all of those machines and could blow 'em up."

"How in the world could you drain the ocean dry?" an onlooker inquired incredulously.

"Look," Rogers replied, "I came up with the idea. Now, you guys figure out how to get it done."

> "The longer I live, the more I am certain that the great difference between the feeble and the powerful, between the great and the insignificant is energy—invincible determination—a purpose once fixed, and then death or victory. This quality will do anything that can be done in this world."
>
> — SIR THOMAS BUXTON

In his unforgettable manner, Will Rogers described the plight of so many big dreams (and would-be dreamers). Coming up with ideas and standards is the easy part. Putting together an action plan—your HOW—is difficult.

At the end of this chapter, you will have the opportunity to put together an action plan to help you reach your primary goals. Corporations refer to this stage as writing a business plan. A business plan can be quite complex; your personal goals should be simple and direct.

How do you develop a plan to reach your goals? Think through the steps required to get where you want to go. And don't forget to include brief strategies and important changes that may affect your action plan.

 Your WHEN

You should set a time and date for completing your goals. In other words, they should be measurable. What cannot be measured will never be performed, so if you want to start reaching mileposts up the road, give yourself definite deadlines for reaching them. Then hold yourself to those deadlines.

Things change, of course. Sometimes circumstances may force you to alter your timetable. What doesn't change is that without a timed and dated set of goals—your WHEN—your chances of reaching those goals are reduced considerably. Your timetable should also be closely tied to your long-term, intermediate, and short-term goals.

If specific goals are so crucial to success, why don't more people use them? Some of the reasons include:

- Fear of moving outside one's comfort zone. Fear is the path of least resistance. It is easier to stay where I am than to risk failure.

- Poor self-image, or the inability to imagine being successful. Visualization is critical to the successful achievement of goals. (Have you ever noticed the use of before-and-after photos as motivation for diet programs?)

- Skepticism or a failure to buy into goal setting.

- An unwillingness to put in the time and effort to achieve defined results.

- Lack of knowledge about how to set specific, measurable goals.

Goal setting is the most widely endorsed personal development tool in the world today. And it has been proven that success has more to do with goal choices than abilities. It is the measurement that matters. Most of us don't want to measure anything because we don't want to know the truth about where we are. But you can't know the truth of the accomplishments unless you first admit the truth of where you are.

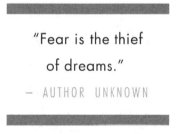

"Fear is the thief of dreams."

— AUTHOR UNKNOWN

Goal setting is also a practical display of faith in God. When you set goals, you say, "Not only do I believe in God, but I also believe that He is going to allow me to be able to purchase this home that costs this much in this neighborhood. I believe that God is going to give me, as a pastor, the ability to reach this many people by this date. I believe that God is going to allow me to reach this quota of sales by the end of this quarter."

Goals start as visions or dreams, and with planning, determination, communication, and focus, they can become reality.

From Vision to Reality

Most people who have achieved phenomenal things sense a divine providence that they are supposed to do it. Whether they are Christians or not, they feel as if nature, God, higher self, or whatever they call it is directing their steps. Their very existence is based upon that providence.

If you listen to Steve Jobs, you quickly see that it has been his mission in life to put a personal computer (preferably with an Apple logo) on everyone's desk.

Your WHY goes far beyond "This is a neat idea," and creates a stick-ability. You can't shake it. You can't get it off of you. That's one of the ways to know that it is from God. Every time you seek the Lord, this idea comes up. "Why is it that every time I pray, God keeps giving me this idea?"

Some people say, "Lord, I need more money." But God keeps bringing up in their mind, "Yes, you can start your own business."

"Yeah, God, that's great," they reply. "But first I need more money."

But have you considered that maybe the Lord isn't going to give you money? That instead He wants to give you the means to earn that money?

We tend to want the payoff without having to create and manage the journey. But God doesn't give us the payoff immediately. He gives us the vehicle—the means—so we do the work, cooperating with Him, to get the payoff.

> "If you have built castles in the air, your work need not be lost; that is where they should be. Now put foundations under them."
>
> — HENRY DAVID THOREAU

Why does God work that way? Why doesn't He just give us what we ask for? Think about it this way: People use people to get tasks done; God uses tasks to get people done. He grew David into a warrior by giving him the task of fighting a bear, then a lion, then

Goliath. He grew Gideon into a leader by giving him the Midianites to fight.

You don't develop on your own. You develop by having a goal bigger than you are. To achieve that goal, you have to become bigger. A goal forces you to become bigger, stronger, and better, and enables you to tackle even bigger goals.

I go back to what the Apostle Paul said: "I can do all things through Christ" (Philippians 4:13, KJV). He didn't say I do all things. He said I *can* do, which means that the *can* is always to be followed by the *do*. You need to be doing something. This is not just a verse you repeat or memorize. It should move you to do something.

Gideon was in the winepress trying to thresh wheat for his family to eat. Are you doing something that God can bless?

God wants us to be active. Never leave the place of decision without taking the first step toward your goal. If you make a decision to do something, you should do something that day about it, even if it is small. You see, God doesn't bless intentions. He blesses actions. Get started today.

Once you start pursuing your goals, you will face obstacles. One of the biggest challenges will be exhaustion. You may become discouraged and find yourself tempted to quit. The book of Galatians tells us, "Let us not become weary in doing good, for at the proper time we will reap a harvest if we do not give up" (Galatians 6:9).

> "Some people must dream broadly and guilelessly, if only to balance those who never dream at all."
>
> — ARTHUR M. SCHLESINGER JR.

God assumes that when you are doing well you will get extremely tired. But that tiredness and exhaustion and thoughts of giving up are part of the price you pay for the harvest. In fact, one of the signs that you are near the harvest is that feeling of exhaustion. Therefore, being tired should not make you quit. Instead, it should make you double your efforts. When you are tired it is often a sign that you are close to reaching your goal.

■ Facing the Impossible

I wonder how many times Gideon must have thought, "I can't do it." The chasm is too wide. Human nature tends to make all of us think that way.

One of the greatest parts of getting a vision, setting goals, and developing an action plan is remembering that we have a resource unavailable to people who don't follow God: "For nothing is impossible with God" (Luke 1:37).

Maturity helps us understand that we eventually need to set goals that are too challenging for us to reach in our own strength. When we do that, then God has to show up.

For example, when I am doing marriage counseling, a list will be developed of all the things that need to be changed with each of the spouses, yet inevitably they reply, "But even if I do all these things, I can't make my wife (or husband) do them."

That's where the "God factor" comes in.

Think about it. If you could make everything happen, why would you need God?

You don't have the power to make other human beings do what you want. You need God to change the situation and the people. And when that person changes, who gets the glory?

> "Don't part with your dreams. When they are gone you may still exist, but you will cease to live."
>
> — JONATHAN SWIFT

When we understand this principle, everything is different. It gets less difficult to lay it all on the line, as when Moses stretched his rod over the Red Sea or when David rushed toward Goliath. All or nothing.

You do what everything inside you is saying not to do, but you do it anyway because you know God has called you to do it. You learn what it means to become a "fool" for God.

Can you imagine Gideon outlining his plan to the men who were willing to follow him into battle? Without the vision, the fleece, the goals, the action steps, how would he have been able to convince them that God would give them victory?

Often, God's ability to turn the impossible into the possible doesn't make sense to anyone else but the Lord and you. That's what God uses. He uses the foolish things to confound the wise.

Why would God use a simple, skinny preacher kid named Billy Graham from North Carolina to go fill stadiums around the world and reach them for Jesus? C'mon. Who would think of doing that? But when God steps in, He specializes in making impossible things possible. Don't forget this as you put together your goals and action steps. The Lord is God of the impossible.

Who Gets the Glory?

As you develop your plan, keep in mind that there are two facets to reaching the goal: God gets the glory and you get the growth.

Growth is not money or fame. We always think that money and fame are the payoff. They aren't. Unless you grow, you will just spend the money. Without growth, the house you buy will just become another house and the car will just become another means of transportation. Money can be spent and fame can be lost, but growth is permanent. The growth that you experience as you move from goal to goal can never be spent or removed.

We always envy people who win trophies. But most trophies sit on shelves collecting dust, rusting, or getting broken. Likewise, fame is fleeting. Even if you are in the newspapers, interviewed on the national news and win every award in your field, by tomorrow you will be old news.

But when you do things God's way, the difference is that you still have the growth that no man can take away. Take away the cameras and notoriety, and you still have the satisfaction that God has helped you grow.

When you plan and achieve your goals properly, God gets the glory and you get the growth. God says, "I've come to make you into the image of My Son." That's the growth. You become more like Jesus. That is the greatest payoff as you learn to seek God's best.

▰ Looking Back—Looking Forward

New vision comes from divine discontent. The children of Israel were not content to be continually harassed by the Midianites and live like animals in caves. The vision Gideon received from God was the solution to Israel's divine discontent with their dire situation.

To achieve great things, you must first admit that you aren't happy with past failures or the way things are. This isn't "positive thinking." The danger of positive thinking is that we take a negative situation and try to act as if it is good. Being positive, in that sense, means that we are lying to ourselves. True positive thinking means that we admit where we are, but we also are grateful that we don't have to stay there.

One of the best examples from history is the story of the Peruvian Railway. South American engineers were called in during the mid-1800s to give their ideas on a possible railroad through the Andes Mountains. These men gathered all the information they could and loudly proclaimed the job "impossible."

Experts from the United States were asked to give their opinions about whether the railroad could follow the River Rimac. Even these men, considered the world's best, claimed that it could not be done.

As a last resort, a Polish engineer named Ernest Malinowski was brought in. His reputation was well known, but he was in his sixties, so the authorities feared to impose such a rigorous task on the man.

Malinowski assured the representatives of the various South American countries that the task was not impossible and that he could complete the job. They awarded him the project, and in 1880 he oversaw the construction of the highest railroad in the world.

The track began in Peru, winding its way across the Andes. Sixty-two tunnels and thirty bridges had to be built. One tunnel was four thousand feet long, built fifteen thousand feet above sea level. Twice, revolutions in some of the participating countries held up construction. Once Malinowski had to flee Peru and remain in exile for a time.

Nothing, however, deterred this aging Polish man from completing the engineering feat that became one of the wonders of the world by the turn of the century.

How about you?

Learning to develop your dream into a panoramic vision is hard enough. Drafting and carrying out a plan of action is even more difficult. That is why so few dreams survive. You hold the key to tomorrow's doors. Your decisions affect your next steps.

Knowing where you are is critical. You can't realize the dream until you admit how far away you are from it. That seems to be the point of Gideon's fleece in Judges 6. We get so caught up in judging Gideon for asking for a sign. In many ways he simply wanted to know where he stood with God—"Is this for real? I'm trying to put together an action plan to accomplish the vision that You have given me, but I really need to know where I stand! Are you there, God?"

Granted, sometimes when we pray for a sign we are merely stalling, hoping for a different vision, looking for a loophole so we don't have to move forward. By his actions, Gideon proved that this wasn't the case. He needed encouragement from the Lord. He needed his level of expectation raised. That is why the fleece is more about encouragement than anything else.

Gideon was saying, "God, I know in my head that You are with me, but I need to know in my heart—in my emotions—that You are sitting beside me, that You are saying, 'I'm with you right now as you...'" The fleece was Gideon's tangible, specific confirmation that "God is with me in this moment." It wasn't just the general "God is somewhere out there" concept.

God has no problem when we get specific with Him. He can change anything at any time, but He has designed us to want to put things into bite-sized dreams and goals.

How about you? What is God leading you to do?

Your life will never be any more successful than your goals. Specific, measurable goals and plans are the way to put solid foundations under your lofty castles. Putting together a specific nuts-and-bolts action plan is vital to your future success.

Remember the ideal equation or formula: Why + What + How + When = Your Successful Master Plan.

Most of all, remember that everything is negotiable, except the mission—what you believe God is leading you to do.

Dreams are a little like riding through a prosperous neighborhood and trying to imagine living in one of the most beautiful homes you see. Setting goals is like picking out one of those homes and promising yourself you will have one just like it by a certain date.

But if that is all that ever happens, you will only wind up frustrated. You might even come to resent the people who have the good fortune to live in those fabulous houses. You see, in addition to having dreams and goals, you must also develop a concrete plan to make your aspirations come true.

You have to become a practical dreamer.

Your plan and subsequent activities will never be any better than the goals on which they are based. Therefore, let me encourage you to set aside a definite time during the next few days to formulate a complete set of goals for every area of your life. Start with long-range goals, and then break them down into intermediate and short-range goals.

Big dreamers set goals for themselves and live by those targets.

You can too.

ACTION PLAN

? First, spend some time in prayer, thanking God for his presence in your life and asking Him for wisdom in making plans that will glorify Him and help you to grow. Then take out your notebook and write down your answers to the following questions. Don't rush through this part. Remember, you're building the foundation for your future success.

1. Your WHY.

Take a few moments to write out your vision statement. What is your WHY. What do you believe that God is calling you to do, be, become? And why do you believe that?

2. Your WHAT.

Take a few moments to write your long-term goals (three to five years), and be sure to define why these results are important to you.

Next, break your long-term goals into intermediate goals (one to two years). What major steps will be necessary to reach your five-year goals? Those are your intermediate goals.

Now, what do you need to do over the next year to reach your intermediate goals? Those are your short-term goals (next twelve months). Write those down.

3. Your HOW.

Take a few moments to put together an action plan to help you reach some of your primary goals. Corporations refer to this stage as writing a business plan. For now, keep it simple and direct.

How do you plan to reach your goals? Write an action plan for each one.

4. Your WHEN.

When are you going to accomplish each of your goals? What are your WHEN deadlines? Remember to be specific.

What will your personal life be like in five years, providing you achieve your overall action plan?

NOW all the Midianites, Amalekites and other eastern peoples joined forces and crossed over the Jordan and camped in the Valley of Jezreel. Then the Spirit of the LORD came upon Gideon, and he blew a trumpet, summoning the Abiezrites to follow him. He sent messengers throughout Manasseh, calling them to arms, and also into Asher, Zebulun and Naphtali, so that they too went up to meet them.

(JUDGES 6:33–35)

STEP SIX

There are only three ways to get anything done:

- Do it yourself.

- Get help.

- Give help.

Each of those ways has its merits, but each is also limiting. Only when you can do all three simultaneously can you begin to understand how to change your world and experience God's best for your life. In fact, your success will depend largely on how effective you are in getting people to help you achieve your goals.

We live in an individualistic society. In our Western culture, most of us tend to believe that we can accomplish our dreams on our own. We tell ourselves (and others):

"I can do it."

"I can handle it all by myself."

"I've got it covered."

"I will just pull myself up by my own bootstraps."

It's not wrong to believe in yourself and take personal responsibility for your own actions. That's a good thing. However, although it is wonderful to believe in yourself, this is not the end-all answer to your success. In order to have success, you will need a team.

> If you want one year
> of prosperity, grow
> grain. If you want
> ten years of prosperity,
> grow trees. If you
> want one hundred
> years of prosperity,
> grow people.

Gideon obviously knew this. When God told him to tear down the altar of Baal, he immediately called in a few of his closest workers. One of the first things he did when he became sure that God had actually called him to battle the Midianites was to put out a call for an army.

Gideon had already had a personal victory. He had already made huge changes in his life. God changed his attitude, his personal character improved, and his prayer life was transformed. Gideon confronted himself and his own family. He confronted his own community. Now he was about to raise an army from the beleaguered nation of Israel.

■ Teamwork

Everyone knows the importance of working together, right? Wrong. Many people, businesses, organizations, and families still don't understand. Take a look at the party politics in Washington or your state capital. Look at the problems of companies or organizations of any size and you will see how far we have to go.

James M. Kouzes and Barry Z. Posner, leadership consultants and best-selling authors, wrote:

> Teamwork is essential for a productive organization. Collaboration is needed to develop the commitment and skills of employees, solve problems, and respond to environmental pressures. Fostering collaboration is not just a nice idea. It is the key that leaders use to unlock the energies and talents available in their organization.

Archimedes once said, "Give me a lever large enough and I can move the world." He was speaking of iron and wood, but leverage is most powerful when used with people.

> "If I have seen further it is by standing upon the shoulders of giants."
>
> — SIR ISAAC NEWTON

The late J. Paul Getty, one of the richest men in history, once said, "If you help enough people get what they want, you will automatically get what you want."

Learning the value of leverage is one of the most important concepts. But getting people to work with you is more than a quick fix—it must be bought with the price of opening yourself to others, trusting them to do a good job, encouraging their growth, and giving them positive reinforcement on a job well done, as Gideon quickly learned.

■ Building the Right Team

But the Spirit of the LORD entered Gideon, and he blew a trumpet, to call the Abiezrites to follow him. He sent messengers to all of Manasseh calling them to follow him. He also sent messengers to the people of Asher, Zebulun, and Naphtali. So they also went up to meet Gideon and his men. (Judges 6:34–35, NCV)

It used to be Gideon alone. Then it was Gideon and a handful of co-workers. Now it was Gideon and thirty-two thousand men. That's quite a difference. Something major was happening to cause that many men to come together to fight against Midian and the eastern tribes.

Something happened to make all these men want to join Gideon. That is the way leadership works. To be able to lead others, you first must prove that you can lead yourself and stand up to others (in this case, against the men of Gideon's town). He now had a massive group of would-be warriors following him.

> One of the best ways to see if you are a leader is to look behind you and see if anyone is following you.

It is important to note that a huge part of being successful is having the willingness to ask for help from others—to be part of a cohesive group. Arrogance says, "I can do this. I don't need anybody. I can do this on my own." The reality is that you can't do it on your own.

We have many examples of teamwork in the Bible. God lives in a community called the Trinity. He is never alone. He is three persons: the Father, the Son, and the Holy Spirit. These persons are all the same God, yet in their diversity they form a bond of unparalleled strength.

God created you to need others too. Adam had Eve. Noah had his family. David had Jonathan. Paul had Barnabas and Timothy. Even Jesus had His disciples. To accomplish great things, you need others.

My Team

As a pastor, I have learned firsthand the power of a team. The first and biggest part of my team is my wife, Jessica. I do not know what I would do without her. Not only is she an amazing wife and mother, but she also has great vision and leadership and is a huge part of our ministry.

After her, I have a phenomenal executive staff that assists me in accomplishing the vision for our church. I spend most of my time either with God or with my team. In fact, as the church has grown, the importance of my team has been the number one key to whether we succeeded or failed at what we were attempting.

Your Team

To take your life to the next level, to experience God's best for your life, you need the right people around you and they need to be on board with your vision. Do you have a team in place? If not, are you ready to build one, using God's strategies?

Anyone who is living abundantly and successfully has a team. They have a team of advisors, mentors, teachers, assistants—all helping and providing input. To do anything remarkable, you need to have a team of people around you.

I want to tell you right now that you are not going to attract a team unless you have something about you that is "attract-able." Gideon had already taken care of his own issues and God gave him favor. That is why people were attracted to him. He had won personal victories. Gideon understood that before he could ask anyone to follow him, he'd better have his act together.

I know people who have amazing dreams, yet they can't even get their own husband or wife on board with them. There is a reason for this, and it is not because the spouses are not supportive. Typically, it is because most people have the same problem that Gideon had. They haven't gotten their own act together.

If people get close to you and choose not to follow you, that means they see something you are not seeing. Or something they see that you are not willing to look at.

If you can discover that problem and then acknowledge it, admit it, and correct it, others will often be willing to follow you. When the people closest to you don't get it, don't want to follow, don't believe in what you feel that God wants you to be, then you need to take a look in the mirror and say, "Okay, what about myself do I need to change?"

Here are a few possibilities:

BE AUTHENTIC

You can never lead someone where you are not willing to go yourself. One way to discover areas of your life that need to change is to play a little game with yourself. If you hired a team of consultants to examine your life what would they tell you to change?

For example, if I were to hire consultants to observe my ministry and examine my leadership, what would they see that I am not seeing? If they followed me for several days, watching how I prepare for messages, how I lead the staff, how I handle conflict and difficulties, how I address counseling needs, how I manage the church's day-to-day operational needs, what would they say to me? What plans would they want me to implement to improve my leadership?

While there may be times when you need a counselor or life coach to help you identify and correct blind spots in your life, often you can identify areas where you need to change by playing the "consultant game." In other words, by looking in a mirror and asking yourself what a counselor might say to you, you remove your emotions from problematic areas. You can step back and take an objective look at your life.

Once you address personal areas needing change, then you can begin to build your team. Once you have examined yourself and identified areas that need change, then it is time to start asking others to help you. But you must first get yourself together so you can ask with credibility. Before people invest in you, they want to know that you are a worthy investment of their time and resources. They want to know that you are *authentic*.

BE TRUSTWORTHY

Do you keep your promises? Fulfill your commitments?

Trustworthiness cultivates credibility. Credibility creates trust. Trust builds strong teams. What would your team members say if someone asked them whether or not you keep your promises? If you don't keep your word, people won't trust you.

Leaders build teamwork and cohesive teams through trust. Trust takes time to build. It must be developed on a day-to-day basis so that it becomes a ready foundation that will stand in the heat of the battle.

If you want to build a team, begin to cultivate a lifestyle of trustworthiness.

BE WILLING TO SHARE YOUR VISION

What is your vision for the future? Do you have one? (Hint: If you wrote down what you want your life to be like in five years, that's a good starting place for developing your vision.)

The dictionary defines vision as a mental image. Effective leaders of organizations know that charters and mission statements cannot fully convey an organization's purpose. So they will develop a vision of the future to represent and communicate their purpose.

Vision inspires people to move beyond what is and to reach for what could be. Vision helps men and women rise above their fears and preoccupations with what can go wrong.

Warren Bennis and Burt Nanus wrote in *Leaders*:

> "A vision is little more than an empty dream until it is widely shared and accepted. Only then does it acquire the force necessary to change an organization and move it in the intended direction."
>
> – BURT NANUS,
> *VISIONARY LEADERSHIP*

A vision cannot be established in an organization by edict, or by the exercise of power or coercion. . . . In the end, the leader may be the one who articulates the vision and gives it legitimacy, who expresses the vision in captivating rhetoric that fires the imagination and emotions of followers who—through the vision—empowers others to make decisions that get things done. But if the organization is to be successful, the image must grow out of the needs of the entire organization and must be "claimed" or "owned" by all the important actors.

Within every organization lies the potential not only for success but also for greatness. These exciting results can only come through a clear vision. But never forget that vision works on a personal level too. Your vision for the future—where you want to be in five years—is key to enlisting people to help you realize that future. But it won't impact others if you keep it to yourself. You have to share it.

BUILD A DEEP SENSE OF PURPOSE THROUGHOUT THE TEAM

Purpose is a statement of what we are here to do or, according to Peter Block in *The Empowered Manager*, "the game we are going to play." The dictionary describes *purpose* as "something one intends to get or do; intention; aim. The object or reason for which something exists."

Simply stated, purpose is an inner, personal reason to succeed.

Goals are wonderful. I think you know by now how much I believe in goals and dreams; however, unless purpose is established first, goals tend to allow hidden conflicts to go unresolved.

Says Tommy Lasorda, manager of the world champion Los Angeles Dodgers and three-time National League manager of the year:

Winning the World Series in 1988 was positive proof of what you can obtain in life if you really believe in yourself. Those twenty-four players got together and all believed in themselves, and what they did showed. It captured the hearts of America because it showed that it is not always the strongest man that wins the fight. In most cases it's the one who wants it just a little bit more than the next, and that's what this team did. They wanted it more.

Infusing people with a purpose clarifies the direction in which you want to move and helps them to follow you. What is your inner, personal reason to succeed? Why do you want to respond to God's call to experience His best? What is your purpose?

BE ENTHUSIASTIC ABOUT YOUR VISION

The word *enthused* comes from the Greek words *en theos*, meaning "in God." If God is in you and what you are doing, you can be enthusiastic about building a team to help you fulfill your vision, whether you are a homemaker, Sunday-school teacher, minister, salesperson, CEO, or sanitation engineer. At one point in his life, King David was facing opposition and his people were even talking about stoning him. At that moment, David "encouraged himself in the Lord" (I Samuel 30:6, KJV). In other words, he found his strength and enthusiasm in God and was able to move forward.

Enthusiasm is a characteristic that all champions possess. Mediocre workers could revolutionize their lives with just a dose of enthusiasm. It is undoubtedly one of the great qualities that a leader needs. It is said that nothing great was ever achieved without enthusiasm. Your enthusiasm projects more about your sincere belief in your leadership abilities than any other single characteristic.

> "Life is a romantic business. It is painting a picture, not doing a sum; but you have to make the romance, and it will finally come to the question of how much fire you have in your belly."
>
> — OLIVER WENDELL HOLMES

Above all, as you develop leadership characteristics, don't be afraid to ask for help. James 4:2 says, "You do not have, because you do not ask God." The principle of asking is not only toward God but also toward those He has placed around you.

Many passages of the Bible are about God's provision, but there is a truth about God's provision that you may have missed. When you see God give someone something from heaven, often it is only after they have exhausted their personal resources *and* those around them in a responsible way.

This means that you must first give your all to accomplish your goals and dreams that are from God. Then you must ask others to help you. When you are out of resources, your relationships become your resources. God placed people around you who have the money, the expertise, and the connections to help you accomplish your dreams.

One of the reasons you are limited in resources is to encourage you to build a team. Life was not meant to be lived alone and outside of relationships.

More than anything else, these components—authenticity, trustworthiness, willingness to share your vision, having a deep sense of purpose, and being enthusiastic about your vision—will enable people around you to grow from the inside out. That kind of growth goes far beyond mission statements and sloganeering, for it builds a tenacious, vibrant spirit within your team. That spirit, in the best cases, is true team spirit. Certainly Gideon seemed to know this, and the results speak for themselves.

> "You only live once, but if you do it right, once is enough."
>
> — JOE LEWIS

The Wrong People

Sometimes God asks us to shrink the team before we add to the team (more about this in Step 7). This is terrible. I never enjoy it, and that is why it is called a "burden of leadership." People always want to talk about the perks of leadership but never the burden of leadership. But surrounding yourself with the wrong people can be disastrous.

Let me give you some suggestions for finding the right people instead of the wrong people. Here are people you definitely want to avoid on your team.

FEARFUL, NEGATIVE PEOPLE

When I say fearful and negative, the most obvious is someone who says something can't be done. I think we are going to do this or that in our company or in our ministry and there is always someone who says, "Yeah, we tried that one time and it didn't really work. Back in 1978 we tried it and it failed, and I don't see it happening."

There is always someone like that. On occasion there is some validity to what the person is saying, but if he or she consistently downplays every idea you have, then the person is probably just negative. Also, remember that negative people attract other negative people. Wolves run in packs.

Another example is if someone comes up to you and says, "Now look, I am worried about you, because *everyone is talking...*" This is usually a smoke screen to cover the fact that *they are the ones doing the talking*.

Negative people oftentimes are also fearful. Many fearful people will tell you that you won't be successful, but they are only projecting their fears onto you. Do not surrender God's agenda or your life to fearful people's doomsday prophecies.

PEOPLE LACKING COMPETENCY IN SKILLS

Let's be real honest: There are some areas of our lives where we know we need to raise the bar—to raise the standard—personally and professionally. Yet the reason we usually do not raise the standard is because we know good and well that some people around us just won't make the cut. This is a hard truth, but many times we will not raise the bar because a certain person will give us all kinds of problems.

"If I raise the bar, they are not going to like this or that." "If I raise the bar I am going to have big problems with my family." Those just are not good enough reasons to not raise the bar. If it is for the cause of Christ and the direction that God is leading you, then you must set high standards. Gideon was

> "Some people like people who win. Some people hate people who win. But people who win will never go unnoticed."
> — MIKE KRZYZEWSKI

willing to raise his standards, those of his family and in his town, and finally those of a whole nation.

Maybe God wants you to set higher standards for your family, or how you handle your finances, or what you do with your leisure time. Maybe He's calling for higher standards in your ministry. You may have to make some unpopular decisions, but if you are to become a leader to those around you, that sometimes is part of the process.

As a church leader, I know there are people who absolutely love our church, and I know there are people who don't. The truth is that if you have no one getting mad at you, then your vision is too broad. The more focused your task, the more people will love it—and hate it. What I am trying to tell you in a nice way is that the greater the success you have, the more rejection you will also receive. You have to be comfortable with both.

The Right People

I have discussed some of the characteristics of people who are wrong for your team. Let's quickly move to the positive—people who are great teammates:

FAITH-FILLED AND POSITIVE

When Gideon was assembling his army, God said to tell the men who showed up, "If you are afraid to go into battle, go home now."

Why would they be afraid? There is only one reason that they would be afraid: They didn't have the faith that God was going to give them the victory when He already promised that He was. In addition, fearful soldiers were negative, thinking they might get killed.

If you really don't believe you are going to have victory, then you won't. You show me what you believe in, and I will tell you how well you will do. If you don't have the faith to believe, the victory will never happen. Thus, you always want to surround yourself with faith-filled, positive people—people who have a "nothing is impossible with God" perspective.

PREPARED AND COMPETENT

Your teammates also need to be battle-ready. They need both confidence and competence. You want to find people for your team who have proven themselves in past experiences. One way to know if you want a certain person on your team is by looking at his or her personal life, family relationships, and personal finances. Is that person's life in order? Are they following God's leading in their life? Do they appear to be experiencing God's best? If so, then that's the kind of person you want to ask to help you along the way.

> Teamwork is the ability to work together toward a common vision, the ability to direct individual accomplishment toward organizational objectives, and the fuel that allows so-called common men and women to produce uncommon results.

TEAM PLAYERS

In Judges 7:4–6, God tells Gideon that he needs to reduce his team even further. So He instructs Gideon to let the men go down to the river to drink. Then He says, "Hey, look at the men who got down and put their face in the water to drink. We need to let them go." Here are a bunch of guys who got down in the water. If a soldier puts his head in the water, can that soldier be looking out for the enemy? Can they be watching your back if they are looking at the water the whole time? No way! This type of soldier is always saying "What's in it for me?"

The real soldiers—only 300—got on one knee, continued to look around, to be aware of their surroundings, and lapped up a little water.

What were they doing? They were staying alert because they knew there was an enemy nearby and they were battle-ready. They were saying, in effect, "I don't care if I am drinking water; I have my sword in my hand and I am ready."

The guys who had their heads in the water would be dead if they were attacked by surprise. Anyone in the military knows that you have to keep your eyes open. You never take your eyes off the enemy—never! You have to be battle-ready. Good soldiers want to secure the perimeter before getting a drink. If one guy is down lapping up water, the others can be looking out for the rest of them. I am watching the perimeter. They are drinking, so I am watching for them. That is a team player. It is not about me. It is about the team. Those are the kind of people that you want on your team.

ONBOARD WITH THE VISION

Not only were these 300 soldiers left on board with the vision, but they also understood that this was a battle. They understood Gideon's vision and knew that the mission would not be accomplished until the Midianites were lying around them dead—not wounded, but dead!

There comes a time in everyone's life when the price has to be paid to take life to the next level. One of those prices is to examine your vision and make sure your team is on board with it.

Perhaps you have been putting off a difficult discussion with someone. In a ministry, you may have to look fellow laborers in the eye, challenge them to get on board with your vision, and ask them to step down if they can't support you. In a personal relationship, maybe you need to lovingly confront a spouse or a child.

Pray. Then confront, if necessary, always in love.

One last word of advice—never beg someone to stay on your team. If team members choose to leave, then let them go. Sometimes God will have someone come onto your team, company, or ministry for a season, but when that season ends, it is time to move on. There is no reason to look at this as a failure. It may just be time for that person to move on. It happens. When it happens, regroup and know that God will refill the hole created by a sudden departure.

God is bigger than your needs. Trust Him, and love people even when they are leaving. If someone is on the way out, don't drag it out. Make the transition quickly so both of you can move forward. Many times God will prepare you for your next chapter in life by creating some exits for others whom He does not intend for you to keep.

Remember the key to Gideon's victory was not the certain people he had with him, but those he did not have with him. I would rather have a few loyal, battle-ready soldiers in my army than a big mass of uncommitted, disloyal people.

It is one of the prices you must pay as you learn to seek God's best.

Looking Back–Looking Forward

Three men were at a worksite laying brick. All three had exactly the same tools, mortar, and materials. Yet they looked different as they worked. An observer went to each one.

"What are you doing?" the questioner asked the first worker.

"Layin' brick," the laborer grumbled. "It's a paycheck, even if it is hard work."

"What are you doing?" the observer asked the next man.

"Well," the second worker replied, "I'm one of the construction people, and we are putting together the east wall of a structure."

"What are you doing?" the questioner asked the third worker.

"I'm helping to build a cathedral." The worker wiped his brow and spoke excitedly. "And someday, right where we are standing," he gestured toward the construction site, "spires will rise high above us, and people will be meeting to worship, to seek peace, to find God, and be educated."

The first worker held a job. The second man had acquiesced to common goals. The third man was a team-builder with a powerful purpose and vision—he was a shining example of letting his life be driven by a plan and learning to seek nothing less than God's best.

ACTION PLAN

? Building a team is a key part of finding and experiencing God's best for your life. Depending on your needs and goals, that team will take different shapes. It may be made up of family members, friends, coworkers, fellow church members, mentors, or teachers. Remember that the goal of a team is to increase your available resources so that you can effectively accomplish what God is directing you to do.

Take some time to pray and ask God about the team you should build. Then open your notebook and write down answers to the following questions:

1. How good are you at team-building? List three of your strengths.

2. List three of your team-building weaknesses that need improving.

3. What specific steps must you take to get better at team-building?

4. List three people you might ask to be on your team and why you think they can help you follow God's calling.

EARLY in the morning, Jerub-Baal (that is, Gideon) and all his men camped at the spring of Harod. The camp of Midian was north of them in the valley near the hill of Moreh. The LORD said to Gideon, "You have too many men for me to deliver Midian into their hands. In order that Israel may not boast against me that her own strength has saved her, announce now to the people, 'Anyone who trembles with fear may turn back and leave Mount Gilead.'" So twenty-two thousand men left, while ten thousand remained.

(JUDGES 7:1–3)

STEP SEVEN

BE WILLING TO CHANGE YOUR PLANS

An essential step of following God's plan and seeking His best is learning to expect God to change our plans. Gideon learned this as he prepared to face the Midianites.

So far, we've seen Gideon respond to God's call, commit himself to obey, confront his family and town, and put out a call for an army—a team. And the response was huge. When Gideon called for his countrymen to assemble, 32,000 men showed up. So far, so good. The Israelites were still vastly outnumbered, but at least they had a decent army.

You can almost hear Gideon giving his commanders a pep talk. "Sure, there are more than 135,000 well-equipped soldiers there in the valley over yonder. Sure, we are going to have to work hard to transform all our guys from farmers and cave dwellers into mighty warriors. But we can take the Midianites and all those eastern tribes, I promise you!"

Then everything changed. Imagine Gideon's conversation with his deputies after he hears God's updated plans.

"Hey, guys, you aren't going to believe what I just heard from the Lord. He says to tell everyone who is afraid to go home. What do you think of that new plan?"

They were at Mount Gilead when God delivered this instruction. Mount Gilead was the last point where you could still turn around and get away. It had an east exit and a west exit. Once you crossed over the hill of Moreh to the north, you ran headlong into the massive camp of Midian, and you would be in the battle whether you wanted to leave or not.

In other words, Mount Gilead was the point of no return. Once you passed it, it was wartime, not talk time. God gave Gideon's men a choice, saying, "Men, don't give me the talk anymore. Anybody can talk to me about how big and bad you are, but when it comes to fighting, can you deliver?" God was telling them that if they were afraid, they should leave then, because on the other side of the mountain was a real enemy. They would face life or death. It was time for a decision.

> "There is no security on this earth. There is only opportunity."
>
> — GENERAL DOUGLAS MACARTHUR

As a result, 22,000 left. Now, Gideon only had 10,000 men. Somehow, I don't think this was what he would have chosen as a battle strategy.

Then came the clincher: "But the LORD said to Gideon, 'There are still too many men'" (Judges 7:4).

Too Many Men?

Here is the snapshot: 22,000 are trudging over the hill, waving bye-bye and heading home. Only 10,000 remain to take on more than 135,000 of the best soldiers in the world. In any book of warfare, one man against thirteen are not good odds for victory.

But God wanted the odds to get even more absurd.

You know Gideon had to be asking, "Too many men? Excuse me Lord, did you say *too many*? Don't you mean *too few*?"

I don't know about you, but my mind doesn't think like that. When I am going to battle I want more people than the enemy, not fewer. If there was one big bully on the playground when I was a child, I always thought it was nice to have a buddy or two to help me out. It just made good sense and kept me from getting my lights punched out too many times. If I were going up against over 135,000 warriors, I would want 136,000 guys on my side. Wouldn't you?

I wouldn't want 32,000. And certainly not just 10,000.

If you were starting a new business, can you imagine hearing the Lord say, "I am going to help you start that business, but you have too much money and too many resources for that business."

What would you think?

I'm sure I would argue, "No, really, I am fine with this money, Lord, thank You. How about if I keep it just in case something goes wrong?"

As Gideon quickly learned, there are times when God says, "If I give you all the resources you need, how could I prove Myself in your life?"

Vision, goals, an action plan, and a team are great. That is why I spent Step 6 on those vital subjects. However, faith often means that you have to start without having everything perfect. Many times God asks us to start without having all the resources in place, rather than giving us all the resources and more.

"Too many men, Lord?"

I'm sure Gideon did not like the direction the odds were going, but he trusted the Lord. It is a good thing Gideon had already received

> When God is going to do something wonderful He begins with a difficulty. If He is going to do something very wonderful, He begins with an impossibility.

the signs of the offering and fleece, because soon, things were going to get even more incredible.

■ Still Too Many Men

Humanly speaking, the situation quickly went from absurd to completely ridiculous. "Then the LORD said to Gideon, 'There are still too many men. Take the men down to the water, and I will test them for you there'" (Judges 7:4, NCV).

Once again, God decided to weed out the people from Gideon's team who apparently did not match the vision.

I have found as a pastor that many times I get upset when people leave my church for any reason. However, as in this case, God says that we need to trust in His ways, not our ways. He is in charge, not Gideon, not me, and not you.

So God gave Gideon a simple test to further thin out the fighting men.

"If I say, 'This man will go with you,' he will go. But if I say, 'That one will not go with you,' he will not go." So Gideon led the men down to the water. There the LORD said to him, "Separate them into those who drink water by lapping it up like a dog and those who bend down to drink." There were three hundred men who used their hands to bring water to their mouths, lapping it as a dog does. All the rest got down on their knees to drink. Then the LORD said to Gideon, "Using the three hundred men who lapped the water, I will save you and hand Midian over to you. Let all the others go home." So Gideon sent the rest of Israel to their homes. But he kept three hundred men and took the jars and the trumpets of those who left. (Judges 7:4–8, NCV)

In Step 6, I shared about the critical difference between the 9,700 soldiers who fell to their knees and slurped the water directly from the stream, as opposed to the 300 who cautiously cupped their hands and brought the water up to their mouths while watching the other soldiers' backs.

What I want you to notice now is how, when Gideon sent the 9,700 men home, he kept the jars and trumpets that were among those who left. This was an amazing strategy, as we shall see.

The extra trumpets and jars may seem a little ridiculous to us. "Who needs those things?" we would be tempted to say. "We don't need a bunch of leftover pottery and musical instruments. What we need are all the swordsmen who are now heading home."

The resources that we think are useless are often the very things that save us.

> "Success is not measured by what a man accomplishes, but by the opposition he has encountered and the courage with which he has maintained the struggle against overwhelming odds."
>
> — CHARLES A. LINDBERGH

The Band of 300

In short order Gideon's band has been reduced from 32,000 men down to 10,000 and then down to 300. Barely 1 percent of the men who were originally with Gideon remained.

I want to tell you something important—God can do more with 1 percent that is truly obedient than we can ever do with 100 percent in our own strength. In ministry, business, war, and life, people talk big until the crisis comes. But how do they handle themselves in the middle of the battle?

Everyone can sound spiritual at church. I want to know how you handle yourself when someone is telling dirty jokes in the break room. Where is your Christianity then? I want to know how you handle yourself Monday through Friday. What do you do when the pressure is on you?

When you are single, you may talk about honoring God's Word, but where do you take your cues when dating? What do you do when the lights are out? Where is your faith when the pressure is on?

Are you still going to hang on to your marriage when it seems you have fallen out of love? When the battle is fierce, real soldiers rise to the occasion and the play soldiers go home.

Everybody can talk big about reaching the world for Christ until it costs them financially. The point is most people talk big about serving God until it is inconvenient, difficult, frustrating, tiresome, or depletes our personal resources. The people God blesses are those in that small percentage who are really committed to Him.

God asked Gideon to attack the Midianites with only 300 soldiers, about 1 percent of the 32,000 people who were originally willing to fight. The others he had to send home.

■ The Right Soldiers

Gideon had to become what Jim Collins, in his book *Good to Great*, called a "Level 5" leader. Collins writes that the Level 5 leader is someone who recognizes that what is good for the organization is good for the leader. The sooner a person learns that lesson, as either a team member or a team leader, the sooner he or she can deal with the harsh realities of organizational changes.

It doesn't matter what feels good emotionally. A Level 5 leader will fire his brother-in-law if it is best for the company. Jesus did what was best for the kingdom of God and it cost His life on the cross. He was willing to do that.

Gideon did what was best for the nation of Israel, even though it seemed ridiculous.

If you're in a place of leadership, you have got to be willing to face the hard facts when it comes to building your team and getting the job done (or in this case, getting the war won!). You have to be willing to raise the bar even if not everyone is able to cut it. This is painful to do. This is the most difficult thing I have to do in ministry. It is the most difficult thing you will do in your life.

If you're a parent who feels God calling you to be a godly leader to your children, you may have to look at your family's lifestyle and make hard decisions about what needs to change.

Maybe you're a teen who feels called into ministry but your friends think your choice is silly. Are you going to be willing to set the bar high for yourself and for others? Are you willing to put up with the criticism to be used by God?

It is painful to say, "Here is the way we are going. God has called us in this direction. This is how we are going to do it. Now, are you ready to get with the program?"

It is said that Alexander the Great, upon learning of a cowardly soldier in his army who also was named Alexander, sternly told the young man, "Stop being a coward or drop that good name." The lesson is clear. The message to all believers is the same today. We must faithfully strive to live up to all that the name "Christian" implies.

Whether you're leading a corporation, a family, or just a group of friends, if you want to build an incredible team, you have got to be willing to set standards that not everybody can keep. If you want to build an incredible sales force, it means not just hanging out with your best salesman, but may mean correcting and even getting rid of the ones who are not selling.

God said, "If you are not going to fight, go now!"

In retrospect, I believe it was a loving move. Sometimes God directs us to shrink the team before we add to the team. This is so difficult and I never enjoy it, but that is one of the burdens of leadership. People always want to talk about the perks of leadership but never the burden of leadership. Both are part of the job.

Excitement in the Midst of Change

Now that God has winnowed Gideon's army down to a mere 300, He graciously gives Gideon one final sign to strengthen his resolve. He tells Gideon and his servant to sneak down to the Midianites' camp at night and listen to what the enemy is saying. Look what happens when Gideon goes down there:

> When Gideon came to the enemy camp, he heard a man telling his friend about a dream. He was saying, "I dreamed that a loaf of barley bread rolled into the camp of Midian. It hit the tent so hard that the tent turned over and fell flat!" The man's friend said, "Your dream is about the sword of Gideon son of Joash, a man of Israel. God will hand Midian and the whole army over to him!" (Judges 7:13–14, NCV)

Gideon overheard one of his enemies talking about him, referring to the "sword of Gideon" and the great victory that Gideon was going to have over them. My favorite part of this scripture is the way the enemy soldiers refer to Gideon's sword, yet to our knowledge, based on what we read in the Word, Gideon does not have a sword! Gideon's reputation begins to become bigger than he feels about himself. When you take bold actions, your reputation begins to precede you.

Gideon evidently made such an impression by being willing to confront the hard issues and the hard people in his life that his reputation had grown. Now there were literally nations that were afraid of him.

Are you willing to be part of something bigger than yourself?

Are you willing to have your dreams and goals changed as you learn to follow God's vision for your life?

You build a reputation not by great intentions, but by great actions.

Amazing things can happen when you discover that God wants to use you, but first He has to see if you will be obedient. As a result of Gideon's obedience, within days God took a meek wheat thresher hiding in a winepress and turned him into truly a mighty man of valor whose reputation was running rampant through the fiercest army of its generation.

Even more amazing, Gideon's "head cheerleader" was a Midianite soldier!

Imagine what Gideon thought when he heard himself described. You see, when God is moving in your life, even your enemies end up speaking encouragement into your life.

Whenever someone speaks badly of you, do you ever think of the encouragement in their words? Most of the time, people tend to put others down because they feel threatened by them. They build themselves up by putting you down. But they probably wouldn't feel the need to do that if there weren't qualities in your life of which they were envious. If you think about it, this is encouraging if you see it in the proper light.

We all need encouragement, even if it is from the enemy camp. Every one of us needs encouragers in our lives. Even if the enemy means it for evil, God can use it as encouragement.

What does this have to do with a chapter on being change-friendly, of being willing to change plans as God directs? When you are out on the cutting edge, you need to take encouragement from wherever you can get it.

When we deal with difficult people or problems, God will use that to focus us and encourage us as we go through the changes. Gideon's enemy was the one who encouraged him to go fight them. God can use anyone, even your enemy.

> "I love the man that can smile in trouble, that can gather strength from distress, and grow brave by reflection."
>
> — THOMAS PAINE

Maybe you have someone like that at work who enjoys, even relishes, talking badly to you or about you. They may say things that are not true. They may always be knocking your ideas or complaining to the boss about you. Gossip happens in any setting, and it usually is not positive. People like to belittle other people and talk about how horrible they are.

When this happens to you, you need to take encouragement, because the only reason that person talks bad about you in the office is because they know you are making them look bad. They know you have what it takes or they would ignore you. You are getting your job done, and it is intimidating them.

So it was with Gideon.

Notice that God didn't give Gideon a completely new plan. God didn't bring back a bunch of the old soldiers or infuse Gideon with a bunch of money and say, "Okay, now go and attack." All God did was add encouragement.

You can have a desperate situation, and all you need to do is add a little encouragement and everything changes. Just a little bit of encouragement makes all the difference in the world, especially in the midst of change.

What happened to Gideon after he learned of his enemies' fear?

Gideon got excited and responded to God's encouragement by worshipping Him: "When Gideon heard about the dream and what it meant, he worshipped God. Then Gideon went back to the camp of Israel and called out to them, 'Get up. The LORD has handed the army of Midian over to you!'" (Judges 7:15, NCV).

When is the last time you had personal worship? I'm not talking about the last worship service you experienced at church, but personal time just worshipping God. Never discount the power of worship to the one true God, especially as you go through crisis and change.

When we worship God, we are filled with His presence, power, and passion. Once we have worshipped, we must remember that our worship is incomplete without active obedience that should follow worship.

An Encourager in the Midst of Change

Every one of us needs someone to encourage us, especially during the moments of great crisis and change. However, not only do we need encouragement, but we also need to be encouragers. Look at what Gideon did: "He returned to the camp of Israel and called out, 'Get up! The LORD has given the Midianite camp into your hands'" (Judges 7:15).

In the midst of change, it is important to know that God often places you in a situation because you are supposed to be an encouragement to others. Encouragement is something you can do any time, any place. Proverbs 3:27 tells us to "not withhold good from those who deserve it, when it is in your power to act," so I suggest this also means do not withhold good words when it is in your power to speak.

As Gideon and his men would quickly discover, those encouraging words, confirming what God was planning to do, made all the difference in the world.

> "Flatter me and I may not believe you. Criticize me and I may not like you. Ignore me and I may not forgive you. Encourage me and I will never forget you."
> — JOHN MAXWELL

■ Stronger Vision for Victory in the Midst of Change

What happens next is so practical that it's easy to miss the implications for us today. Gideon is excited because God has given him a vision for victory: "Gideon divided the 300 men into three groups. He gave each man a trumpet and an empty jar with a burning torch inside" (Judges 7:16, NCV).

Making changes as the time for battle nears is one thing, but this was very significant. Now I don't know about you, but if I go into battle, I am not interested in someone handing me some trumpet and a jar! Spare me the Crock-Pot, okay? Give me a weapon. I don't want to "Tupperware" the enemy to death!

So what's with the jar, torch, and trumpet, you ask?

Answer: a workable plan, albeit with unexpected changes!

> "Don't find a fault, find a remedy."
>
> — HENRY FORD

As we discussed in Step 5, it is important to have a plan. If you want God to take you to the next level, you have to understand where He wants you to go. Remember, God never rewards mere intentions; God rewards your actions. Results never happen from the best of intentions. Results happen because you got a vision from God, created a plan, and worked it.

Nevertheless, we have to be willing to allow God to change the plan as He directs. As Gideon and his band of 300 quickly discovered, miracles often happen in the midst of change—if we are willing to be obedient to God's leading.

Leadership by Example

Gideon and his soldiers were on a need-to-know basis. At the appropriate time, God told Gideon what to do. Then, when the time was right, Gideon relayed the information to his men.

As the moment of battle approached, Gideon divided the 300 men into three groups. He gave each man a trumpet and an empty jar with a burning torch inside. Then he said to the men, "Watch me and do what I do. When I get to the edge of the camp, do what I do" (Judges 7:17, NCV).

Gideon said, "Watch me and do what I do."

Can that be said of you and me? Could people emulate our lifestyle and be more effective? Could it be that if everyone in your home watched you and imitated you, then your family life would be amazing? If people at work just did what you do, would your work environment improve? Or would it tank the whole operation if everyone emulated you?

Following God on a need-to-know basis is a challenge, isn't it? Gideon understood the principle of leadership. He had been willing to follow God by faith, even when it didn't make sense, humanly speaking. Gideon's men had seen him in action. Now they were willing to do the same with him.

You cannot ask people to go somewhere you are not willing to go. Gideon led by example.

More Changes

Gideon then said, "When I get to the edge of the camp, do what I do. Surround the enemy camp. When I and everyone with me blow our trumpets, you blow your trumpets, too. Then shout, 'For the LORD and for Gideon!'" (Judges 7:17–18, NCV).

When the Bible offers the phrase "For the LORD and for Gideon!" it may be easy to say, "Oh, okay. Now it is all about Gideon. When did Gideon cut into the Lord's space here? What's going on with that?"

Just remember what had happened in the enemy's camp. God "humbles and he exalts" (1 Samuel 2:7). He places people in leadership for a reason, and it often has little to do with human reasoning. Gideon's name by that time had apparently become an issue for the enemy. His name alone was intimidating. That is why the soldier said, "Oh no! We're going to be handed over to Gideon and his big sword!"

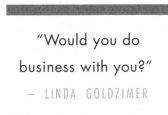

"Would you do business with you?"

— LINDA GOLDZIMER

Remember, to our knowledge, Gideon didn't even have a sword, yet the enemy was afraid of him. His name had become a powerful factor. His reputation had preceded him. The name Gideon had become a potent weapon. By instructing the soldiers to say, "For the LORD and for Gideon!" Gideon was using his name and reputation in a positive way for God.

How can your name be used? When people say your name, do they think of quality or do they think of a lack of quality? Do they think of someone who always does it the right way, or someone who always does it the easy way? Do they think of someone they can trust, someone with integrity, or do they think of someone who's going to go find a way to compromise and produce shoddy work?

God's name is above all names, but your name also must mean something. Whether you like it or not, you have to recognize that your name is attached to other key words that describe your character.

When the soldiers were told to yell, "For the LORD and for Gideon!" in effect they were giving vocal testimony to what God had called Gideon to do. His name meant "we are not afraid to confront the hard issues, and you Midianites are not going to boss us around anymore." Gideon stood up for what was right locally, he faced his own family, tribe, and community, and now he and his men were taking a stand on a national level—to fight for Israel's existence and freedom.

If God has given you a good reputation in your organization, in your church, in your family, use it for serving the greater good and not to serve yourself. Gideon was allowing the name that God had given him to be used for His work, not for his own gain and not for the perks.

Beyond Name Tags

Some people never make a name for themselves because they are not willing to take a risk or work a plan. These people often go for the name tag instead.

We have a lot of name-tag people in the world. Do you know any name-tag people? "Well, you know, I'm the official (fill in the blank) around here." They are quite willing to tell you about what they are in charge of.

I discovered long ago that titles are just that—name tags. I am not concerned about someone's title. I am much more interested in what that person is doing effectively.

God doesn't give titles. He gives functions, as in Ephesians 4:11— "It was he who gave some to be apostles, some to be prophets, some to be evangelists, and some to be pastors and teachers." Paul never insisted that people call him by some long title, but few questioned his calling, authority, or function.

If you have a unique gift and passion for something, you don't need someone else's badge of approval to do it. If you have the gift, you have the authority of God. Gideon obviously had a gift of leadership, a military prowess that he previously didn't even know he had. Now God was about to use it.

When Gideon told the men to yell, "For the LORD and for Gideon!" he certainly wasn't saying, "It's all about me, guys. I'm the man." No, he was saying, "Look, if my name lends any credibility to this, then great. Let's roll."

The lesson is clear. In the midst of change and challenge, each resource becomes invaluable. Use every resource you have. If one of the resources you have is your name, then use it.

Gideon did. The men did. And what happened during the next moments would change the destiny of nations.

Changes and You

Based on current trends, it looks like the future will be more unpredictable than ever, much more so even than many so-called experts are forecasting. Many organizations and individuals, relying on what they have always done before, simply will not outlast the turbulence. Financial, technological, and marketplace changes will come quicker and even more furiously, and only the most flexible people and organizations—those who can learn to change quickly and live with the tumult—will survive.

This was true in Gideon's day. It is even more so today. In the midst of chaos and great change, there will be those who will not only survive but also flourish, despite the obstacles. Are you ready for the changes that are coming? In what ways are you prepared to adjust to the changes?

Gideon certainly learned to change as he followed God's direction. Left to "natural" inclinations, Gideon might have taken 32,000 hastily trained, recently recruited farmers into battle against 135,000 battle-hardened warriors. If you were placing odds on that battle, what would you have anticipated?

But God was in control. Gideon and his men were willing to listen and obey, even in the midst of unthinkable changes and plan revisions.

Truth be told, we don't always have a choice whether or not to accept change. Even when God places a vision before us and helps us put together an action plan, things change. God changes things. The enemy changes things. Even the weather changes things. And in the midst of change, we must trust God to help us supernaturally. That, in a very real way, was the ultimate secret to Gideon's success.

Change-Friendly Champions

Change is inevitable. It can be vitalizing. It is as much of life as breathing in and out. Recognizing the importance and need for change is the mark of a healthy person. In fact, one who truly understands this concept will be invigorated by the possibilities that would never come any other way.

"Eureka!" moments seldom involve new information. Almost always they come in the midst of crisis and change, as plans are altered.

Gideon could have quit and stomped back to the winepress when God started changing what already seemed like a shaky plan: 32,000 against 135,000. People around him would have certainly understood if Gideon had walked away when God reduced the number to 10,000. Most observers probably wondered why Gideon remained faithful when God dropped the number to a mere band of 300.

But because Gideon had a quickly growing confidence in God, boosted by the signs God had given—the offering consumed by fire, the wet fleece, the dry fleece, the words of his enemies overheard—when the moment for war came, he was ready. The often-changed plan was in place. Life, as Gideon and the Israelites knew it, hung in the balance.

We all can learn to be open to change. We can learn from the past and maintain a clear view of the future. We must anticipate and enjoy change. Only then can we move forward into the supernatural victories in store for each of us as we learn to seek nothing less than God's best.

▄▄▄ Looking Back–Looking Forward

There is an old Spanish proverb: *"No es lo mismo hablar de toros, que estar en el redondel."* The English translation goes something like this: "It's not the same to talk of bulls as to be in the bullring."

Gideon and his band of 300 went through many changes on the road to the moment when God's "crockery, torch, and trumpet" plans exploded around the Midianites.

Though they believed they would be victorious, they could not have known—even in their wildest dreams—what would happen next.

An old military axiom says, "No battle plan survives contact with the enemy." As we have discussed throughout this book, it is important to have a vision, goals, and an action plan. However, in the midst of changes, you cannot be a slave to the plan you wrote down on paper.

Sure, going through any crisis or change involves great risk. American overcomer and author Helen Keller once wrote, "Security is mostly a superstition. It does not exist in nature, nor do the children of men as a whole experience it. Avoiding danger is no safer in the long run than outright exposure. Life is either a daring adventure or nothing."

When you face whatever comes against you in the bullring of life, flexibility is the key. Critical adjustments in the midst of the battle are vital to long-term success.

Gideon and his warriors knew this. Their plans were changed again and again as God prepared them for the moment of battle. They were obedient, even in the midst of unanticipated changes.

These are the great lessons we can learn from Gideon's life as we continue seeking God's best for our lives.

ACTION PLAN

? Spend a few minutes in prayer, thanking God for the changes He's brought into your life. Then take out your notebook and write down some answers to the following questions:

1. What areas in your life have changed the most in the past year?

2. What have these changes meant for your life?

3. What can you do right now to help prepare for unanticipated changes?

4. If you follow through on the goals and plans you're making as you work through this book, what changes might you anticipate in the coming year?

WATCH me," [Gideon] told them. "Follow my lead. When I get to the edge of the camp, do exactly as I do. When I and all who are with me blow our trumpets, then from all around the camp blow yours and shout, 'For the LORD and for Gideon.'" Gideon and the hundred men with him reached the edge of the camp at the beginning of the middle watch, after they had changed the guard.

(JUDGES 7:17–19)

STEP EIGHT

Many people desire to break the cycle of failure. They want to discover God's direction and experience nothing less than His best for their lives. They commit themselves to change and even develop a plan. Yet when you find them six months or a year later, nothing has changed. They are still caught up in their original cycle of failure. Why? There can be many reasons, but most likely it's because they failed to put their plan in motion. They failed to take decisive action.

When we last saw Gideon, he and his men were on the cusp of victory. But victory would not be automatic. Gideon and his army of 300 had to take on the massive, intimidating Midianite army. It would have been very easy for them to back down and walk away—especially when they heard Gideon's battle plan.

The instructions were clear, if puzzling, yet too much had already happened for the remaining men to question their commander. Everything he had done had gone against human reasoning and military training.

The men breathed as one. Each knew the possibilities. In some ways, nothing in the plans made sense. Their numbers were too small. They had no experience against such a large army. There was not enough sword power, even before when they had started out with 32,000 fighters. For some reason, that relatively small number

> "Imagination is more
> important than
> knowledge."
>
> — ALBERT EINSTEIN

had gone through a series of tests that ended up whittling the number down to what seemed like a handful.

All of this made the fact of being armed with trumpets, empty pitchers, and torches even more ludicrous. They were too limited, yet it was apparent that the men believed what Gideon had told them. Their leader's words burned through the hearts of each warrior: "Our LORD has given the Midianite camp into your hands!"

How was it possible?

Only 300 men against the entire camp of more than 135,000 well-equipped, fierce soldiers?

Imagine each man's thoughts as the band of 300 moved swiftly into position. It was the beginning of the middle watch, just as the Midianites and their allies had posted it. The sentries apparently never noticed what was happening just out of earshot as the men moved stealthily.

Word was whispered around the huge and widening circle of Hebrew men that everyone was in place all around the Valley of Jezreel. Wordlessly, as if invisible in the night, everyone checked to make sure the torches inside the clay pitchers were lit.

We can only wonder what was going on in each man's mind. Hearts pounded. Men prayed to be brave, no matter what happened next. Though they were a band of fighters who had grown close during the past few days, each knew that he stood alone in the night. Each soldier also knew, without a doubt, that God alone would make the difference between life and death during the coming moments.

They had come too far to turn back or run. The moment of battle approached quickly. Each man stood, trumpet and clay pitcher in hands, ready for whatever would happen next.

Suddenly the sound of Gideon's trumpet pealed through the night.

An instant later, 300 trumpets sounded all the way around the Midianite war camp. The earpiercing sound was deafening, shattering the peaceful sleep of the slumbering enemy army.

The battle cry that followed was even more deafening. "A sword for the LORD and for Gideon!"

Next, a bizarre sound roared through the valley, as if thousands of clay bricks were smashing together. Immediately, a ring of blinding lights illuminated the absolute bedlam that filled the massive camp.

What took place during the ensuing moments became one of the greatest, most startling moments in recorded military history.

More important, what happened to Gideon and his soldiers—if we can comprehend and apply the lessons they learned—can make all the difference in the world for you and me in a world where we sometimes face even greater odds.

Timing Is Everything

It is significant that Gideon began his attack just after the changing of the guards. Changing guards means that Gideon was concerned about the timing of what he was doing.

You may have the right words, the right people, and the right strategy, but if you have the wrong timing, nothing will work right. Timing is everything.

It is that way in everything, certainly in the ministry.

A pastor friend called me this past summer. He was clearly frustrated. "Church is going so badly," he said. "Our ministries are down. Our attendance has been terrible."

I said, "Hey, it's July. Don't count on high attendance in July."

Judging how your church is doing in July is similar to the Disney people judging their numbers in September. There are prime seasons and out-of-season times. Everything has a season.

I told the pastor, "Don't make decisions now concerning what your church is going to do next, because you will be basing your

> "It is not death that a man should fear, but he should fear never beginning to live."
> — MARCUS AURELIUS

decisions on failure, not success. Make decisions when you're on the upswing, never when you're on a downswing."

So many people lose out in life because they make decisions either just before the victory or immediately after a big loss. Neither is the right time for strategic planning. People who win in life make their decisions when they are cranking up.

Likewise, don't make any decisions in your marriage during bad times. My wife, Jessica, and I made a clear choice that we were going to be married the rest of our lives, and we made that decision at the peak of our emotional love, our courtship. I don't think you can get higher emotions than when you're engaged, can you? My love has deepened for my wife and the emotions are still there, but the depth of it changes things. It makes it better, not worse. Regardless, we made the decision on the way up that we would stick together even if we hit hard times. I can honestly say that the decision we made has helped get us through the "wheels-off" times that happen with any marriage, including ours.

Don't make decisions at the wrong time. Timing is everything.

Gideon and his band of soldiers understood the value of timing. The guards were changing. The first-shift guards had been up half the night, keeping watch. The second-shift guards had just been awakened, so they were undoubtedly groggy and tired. None of them were ready. This was the most opportune time to attack the Midianites.

An "Outside-the-Box" Battle Plan

What happened next is a reminder to you and me that following God's will effectively and successfully often requires creative, "out-of-the-box" thinking.

On the surface, the concept was preposterous. On one side were 300 would-be warriors armed with trumpets, clay pots, and torches. On the other side were the fiercest and best-trained 135,000 soldiers in the known world.

Obviously there was more than meets the eye when it came to the weapons of choice: trumpets and clay pottery with torches inside. Let's take them one at a time, starting with the horns that the men blew.

TRUMPETS

In the history of warfare, when you blow the trumpet, the soldiers know it is time to go to battle. Even modern armies have buglers who blow the trumpets for different occasions.

Imagine a field full of soldiers. Because of basic logistics and proven ancient military strategies, leaders used one trumpet for each 1,000 men in order for most to hear the signals clearly.

When you think about it, Gideon's plan was so simple and effective that it remains mind-boggling today. He said, "Hey, let's get a trumpet in the hands of every man." That means the hillsides around the large army of sleeping Midianites and eastern tribesmen had a total of 300 trumpets piercing the air.

If one trumpet was used for each 1,000 men, then 300 trumpets would make the enemy think that 300,000 Israelite soldiers were attacking. What would you think if you were sleeping, trained in the art of war to instantly assess a situation, and you suddenly woke to the blare of 300 trumpets—all sounding simultaneously?

The plan was genius in action. Actually, it was supernatural, far beyond what any human mind could conceive.

TORCHES IN CLAY JARS

Torches have always been a favorite war tactic. There is a natural fear of fire and light when it is used against you. You can illuminate the enemy, making the soldiers vulnerable to attack. And you can use the fire to set the enemy aflame. Either way works well. Armies still use high-tech variations of torches and fire.

Gideon added the element of surprise by keeping the torches hidden inside each man's clay pottery. If the children of Israel had showed

> "History teaches us that in asymmetric warfare the most heavily armed do not always win"
>
> — IGNACIO RAMONET

up with unlit clay pots, it would have taken forever to spread the fire from torch to torch. By that time the Midianites would have killed Israel's band of 300 and headed back to camp for breakfast.

If the torches had been out in the open, the situation would have been much the same. The enemy would have spotted 300 torches from a mile away and had time to prepare for the attack.

As it turned out, the torches were lit and kept inside the clay pots. Remember, each man had a trumpet in his right hand, and in his left hand he held a lit torch hidden in a clay jar. The jars must have been fairly ingenious, for the lid couldn't have smashed against the flame or cut off the oxygen, or the light would have been extinguished. The jars must have been especially tall, somehow allowing the air to come in but no light to escape.

Then, at just the right instant, the men smashed holes in the pottery, turning the hillsides into Yankee Stadium and blinding the enemy.

Go beyond the 300 glaring spotlights. Do you know how loud it must have been to hear clay pots smashed at the same time? Have you ever dropped a heavy piece of pottery? I mean, have you ever dropped a clay pot? Imagine 300 trumpets blaring, followed by 300 simultaneous clay-pot explosions. It must have been utter bedlam.

The chaos would have been overwhelming. No one could have known what was happening in the midst of all the noise. Amid the barrage of noise and commotion, fire and light surrounded them, making them helpless to figure out what was happening.

When all the trumpets were blown at the same time in the middle of the night, then the pots were smashed and 300 flares circled the hillside, two things happened.

The first natural reaction was sheer terror. I don't care how well trained you are—if you were suddenly awakened from a deep slumber and encircled by what sounds like air horns and looks like headlights from a parking lot full of Mack trucks, my guess would be that you might be scared out of your mind too.

The second reaction was not so natural. God clearly stepped in supernaturally to protect His people. In their panic the Midianites and eastern tribesmen picked up their own swords and turned on each other. In the darkness and confusion, they apparently started slicing and dicing without checking the color of game jerseys.

Meanwhile, all around the hilltops, the band of 300 must have been absolutely awestruck to see what happened. We don't know if they had swords or implements of war. All we are told is that they had trumpets, clay pots, and torches.

What a strategy. It translates well even to today's world. When you are outnumbered, you must act bigger than you really are. But what does that mean? It doesn't mean that you are prideful or over-inflated. Acting bigger than you are means you see yourself as God sees you. It means that you are focusing on your strengths, not your weaknesses.

You may be starting a small software company, but if your business card positions you to look like you are in league with Microsoft, you have learned to act bigger than you are. You may not feel very good at being a saleswoman for whatever product you offer, but you can act bigger than you are with an image as polished as if your sales commissions came from Coca-Cola. You may be flipping hamburgers and dipping fries and apple pies, but your attitude should shine as though you might be named president of the entire Burgerama chain just any day.

SWORDS AND STADIUM LIGHTS

"A sword for the LORD and for Gideon!"

Anybody have a sword?

To our knowledge, at least from what we see in Scripture, none of the men had a sword. They had trumpets in their right hands and covered torches in clay pots in their left hands. They didn't stand up, swords raised in the air, yelling, "A sword for the LORD and for Gideon!" They were all too busy holding trumpets and clay pots.

Yet they yelled about the sword for both the Lord and Gideon. What sword were they talking about?

Here is the absolute bottom line, unvarnished and without spin: Even if the 300 men had conducted a surprise attack armed with swords, they might have killed 300 or so of the enemy before the remaining 134,700 Midianites and eastern tribesmen jumped up, grabbed their shields and swords, and made mincemeat of Gideon's little group.

The only weapons that could have worked were the creative ideas that God gave to them. When they had nothing that worked, in terms of human strength and strategy, the children of Israel had to rely on God's creativity.

"Why do people give up big dreams for small realities?"

— KEVIN COSTNER

All they had, in reality, was faith in God's unthinkable plan. They had trumpets and clay pots with fire inside. That's it. But when the moment of truth arrived, the victory God achieved was beyond comparison.

Many times as you seek God's best, you will only have the power of a creative idea at your disposal. Use it, and ask God to bless your idea supernaturally, just as He did with Gideon and his soldiers.

Just as the light was hidden in the clay pots until the right moment, God is waiting to cause the creative ideas hidden deep inside you to explode into the open.

In 2 Corinthians, we are told, "But we have this treasure in earthen vessels, so that the surpassing greatness of the power will be of God and not from ourselves" (2 Corinthians 4:7, NAS).

In other words, we are the jars of clay, covering the light. At the moment of God's choosing, that light can shine through the darkness all around you. Plus, the Bible is clear that God specializes in using broken vessels. People cannot see the light of God in your life until you are broken. It may seem counterintuitive to position yourself as bigger than you are, even as you allow yourself to be broken and humble so the Light of the World can shine through you. But when you understand how much God wants to use you, you will also begin to discover His ways, His strategies.

Creatively Carrying Out His Plan

It is important to look deeper into a part of Gideon's story that we don't often consider. The Scriptures are silent about who came up with the idea for the trumpets, torches, clay pots, and raucous cheer.

We are not told that the angel of the Lord showed up prior to the battle with a detailed schematic of the unusual plan. "All right now, Gideon, here's what I want you to do. Get some trumpets. Get some clay pots. Here's what we're going to do."

You don't see that happening.

We are also not told that God Himself gave the plan.

So who came up with the clay pots and the torches and the trumpet idea? Apparently Gideon did.

This is a monumental lesson. Many believers forget that God gave them a creative mind. In other words, many times God brings you the inspiration, but He wants your perspiration and your ingenuity to carry out His plan. Sometimes we keep asking for miracles while we neglect the fact that one of the greatest miracles in the universe is the human mind—especially when that mind asks for God's direction.

We keep asking for miracles. "Oh God, show up in some burning bush for me, like You did for Moses. Or write a message on

> "When you are completely caught up in something, you become oblivious to things around you, or to the passage of time. It is this absorption in what You are doing that frees your unconscious and releases your creative imagination."
>
> — ROLLO MAY

my garage wall and tell me what You want me to do." We want any kind of miracle.

Remember that David praised the Creator by writing, "I praise you because I am fearfully and wonderfully made; your works are wonderful, I know that full well" (Psalm 139:14). You are the miracle you keep asking for. God wants us to understand that He has already planted the seed—ideas inside us that can change the world.

Yes, you must trust God, but it is also important to know that God wants to trust you. He wants you to use your ingenuity, your creativity. He wants you to think outside the box. But He also wants you to act on your ideas—those incredible, ingenious things that come to your mind all the time. Act on them.

Apparently, Gideon was the one who developed the battle plan. Yes, the inspiration was from God, but Gideon conceived the trumpet, torch, and cheer strategy. Then he went out and put it into practice, along with the help of 300 intrepid followers.

Dream Destroyers

If God has made us all so creative, why don't more people use this creativity to do great things for Him? Often, the main reason we question our God-given ideas is because someone else keeps questioning us, making us lose our confidence.

If you want a limited life, all you have to do is surround yourself with limited people and listen to them telling you all the things you can't do. But if you want an unlimited life—if you want to experience nothing less than God's best—you need to hang out with those who are wise, who walk with the wise, who live unlimited lives, who believe bigger things, who believe God can do more. You need to hang out with people like that.

King Solomon put it this way: "Wisdom is supreme; therefore get wisdom. Though it cost all you have, get understanding" (Proverbs 4:7). If you seek God's wisdom and surround yourself with likeminded people (your team!), He will enable you to do great things with the creativity He has already given you.

Sometimes the most strategic thing you can do is to avoid listening to dream-destroying people. Gideon had a God-given idea, and he ran with it. You will be taking a huge step toward an unlimited life when you learn to trust and nurture the creative ideas that God plants inside your "fearfully and wonderfully made" body, soul, and spirit!

A Lesson in Failure

Although Gideon and his army are our primary focus, at this point in the story the Midianite army provides us with a lesson of what *not* to do.

Terror shattered the night. Gideon's men stayed in place around the camp, and then the inexplicable happened. When Gideon's soldiers blew their trumpets, the Lord put the Midianites and eastern tribesmen in such a panic that they began to fight each other.

If there is a guaranteed strategy for failure and defeat, it is to turn on each other. Whether the self-slaughter happens in your family, church, or business, you will be rendered useless as you fight and destroy one another.

The contrast between the formula for success and defeat couldn't be more dramatic. The soldiers from Israel stood their ground, carrying out their amazing battle plan, while the enemy succumbed to fear and terror, became completely irrational, and started slashing at each other.

> The way I see it, if you want the rainbow, you gotta put up with the rain.

It is easy for me to say this, since I am writing from the cozy comfort of my office. I have subtle lighting, an ergonomic chair, air conditioning, and a glass of water nearby. I am not in the midst of a chaotic scene from a disaster movie, suddenly awakened in the middle of unbelievable noise and overwhelming terror while getting stomped on and slashed by my own buddies.

Nevertheless, the principle is undeniable. To succeed, team players find a way to separate the problem from the person. Teams, co-workers, and families that turn on each other in the heat of conflict or trial, attacking each other without rhyme or reason, are guaranteed to self-destruct.

Accidents happen, especially in situations as terrifying as the moment when Gideon's band of 300 morphed into what appeared to be a 300,000-strong host surrounding the Midianites. However, when friendly fire—soldiers unknowingly killing their own comrades—runs rampant throughout the forces, the battle is over. Turn out the lights. The party is over. You lose.

But when people work together as one cohesive unit, one singular voice, the chances of winning go up immeasurably. Turning on each other almost always guarantees defeat. The lessons are very clear!

What happened next is even more amazing.

The Power of Delegation

The way that you see long-term victories comes only by learning to dispense authority, to gain control and influence by giving up control and influence, to delegate effectively. We see this principle at work in the aftermath of the "trumpet-and-Tupperware" assault.

Judges 7:22 tells us, "The [Midianite] army fled to Beth Shittah toward Zererah as far as the border of Abel Meholah near Tabbath." Now that doesn't mean much to us. We just know this: The enemy cruised. They took off and ran far away.

We don't know how many Midianites and eastern tribesmen survived the initial slicing and dicing at the campground, but some of them were apparently able to run away.

It must have been quite a sight. Imagine hundreds, perhaps thousands of well-trained warriors running through the countryside, scattering like rats when the lights are turned on in the barn.

We already talked about how Gideon's band acted bigger than they really were. That could have taken a turn for the worse. At this

> "Discovery consists of looking at the same thing as everyone else and thinking something different."
>
> — ALBERT SZENT-GYORGYI, NOBEL PRIZE PHYSICIAN

moment, they could have started giving each other high fives, slapping each other's backs, bumping chests, yelling and screaming at each other, and spiking the broken clay pots like running backs in the end zone.

"We're bad! We beat 'em! Anyone else wanna take on Gideon's bad band of 300?"

Can't you see that happening?

Apparently it didn't.

Alabama's legendary football coach, Bear Bryant, used to chastise any Crimson Tide players who celebrated in the end zone by saying, "Don't act like it's the first time you've been there."

We don't know what speech Gideon gave his men, but we do know that we don't read about any premature celebrations among the men. There was still too much to do.

What happened next turned a momentary, miraculous rout into a long-term, life-changing, sustainable victory over forces that had plagued Israel for years:

> Then men of Israel from Naphtali, Asher, and all of Manasseh were called out to chase the Midianites. Gideon sent messengers through all the mountains of Ephraim, saying, "Come down and attack the Midianites. Take control of the Jordan River as far as Beth Barah before the Midianites can get to it." (Judges 7:23–24, NCV)

Gideon teaches us the power of delegation. He sent men to go do the rest of the work and to collect other worker-warriors along the way.

There are four simple phases of leadership that have been successful since ancient times:

- I do—you watch what I do.

- We do it together.

- You do—I watch to make sure it is done right.

- You go do the same thing and mentor others.

This is what Gideon was doing.

Gideon's army chased the Midianites, taking control of the Jordan River before the enemy could get there. The reason the Jordan River was so crucial was quite simple: It was a vital supply line. You need water if you are in war. You need supplies that often can only be delivered quickly by water. Gideon's forces needed to create a perimeter around a critical section of the Jordan.

All of a sudden, it was important for the band of 300 to grow—quickly. Thankfully the other 31,700 soldiers who had been sent home were ready and waiting. Victory cries spread quickly, and a new wave of courage filled the countryside. When you think about it, the call for additional troops provided an opportunity for all the sent-home men to redeem themselves in the eyes of their family and friends.

At the same time, all the additional forces were absolutely necessary for a total victory that would change the region's destiny. It simply wasn't humanly possible to take control of the area without a quick infusion of tens of thousands of reinforcements. The escape routes had to be sealed off. For this, Gideon had to delegate effectively.

> So all the men of Ephraim were called out and they took the waters of the Jordan as far as Beth Barah. They also captured two of the Midianite leaders, Oreb and Zeeb. They killed Oreb at the rock of Oreb, and Zeeb at the winepress of Zeeb. They pursued the Midianites and brought the heads of Oreb and Zeeb to Gideon, who was by the Jordan. (Judges 7:24–25)

Oreb and Zeeb were enemy princes. Granted, we look at princes through the eyes of modern-day people who have watched too many Cinderella-type movies—as if the princes were guys with perfect hair, silken clothing, Spandex tights, and manicured nails.

"These are the hard times in which a genius would wish to live. Great necessities call forth great leaders."

— ABIGAIL ADAMS, IN A 1790 LETTER TO THOMAS JEFFERSON

In actuality, a prince in Gideon's day was the son of a king who was typically raised in the nation's top military school. Princes were trained to become mighty generals by the best strategists and war counselors the king could afford.

There is little doubt that Oreb and Zeeb were the best-educated commanders in the region. Oreb even had a rock named after him and Zeeb had a winepress named after him, sort of like naming a school or highway after a great general today. The two princes must have done well in previous battles to receive these honors. It is noteworthy to observe that the men were killed in the very places that had been named in their honor. Suddenly, instead of those areas being known as places of status and great accomplishments, they were known for defeat. Where once Oreb and Zeeb had dominated, they were killed.

This sent a powerful, in-your-face message to the remaining Midianites that Gideon and the Israelites were no longer afraid of them. For years Midian had intimidated Israel. Gideon's army now said, "We don't fear your once-legendary warriors anymore. You don't intimidate us any longer."

Even though we don't know every detail about the communication between Gideon and his men in the Jordan River sector, we do know that they didn't have modern conveniences like cell phones or the Internet. Therefore, we have to assume that the men in the field had learned well to think on their feet. Gideon delegated effectively, infusing his men with the courage to make such an extraordinarily strategic move as killing Oreb and Zeeb in the places named in their honor.

How does this apply to us?

It is a crucial point, one that will make all the difference in the world, no matter where your "battles" take place—your home, your workplace, or your organizations.

> "You can get anything in life you want, if you will help enough other people get what they want."
>
> — EARL NIGHTINGALE

We like to hold all the authority. It is usually that way from childhood when we play king of the hill and yell, "I'm the big brother, not you!"

Turf building and badge holding come naturally, it seems. The problem is that when we seek to grab and hold onto authority, we eventually lose control. Worse, we lose the opportunity to empower others and thereby impact a larger and larger sphere of influence.

If things get out of control in my home, I know why. And when things are under control, I also know why. Things work best when my wife and I delegate tasks and responsibilities to our children. Otherwise, as any parent knows, bedrooms quickly disintegrate into hazardous-waste dump sites, kids turn into video-playing robots, tempers flare, people yell, parents feel used, doors get slammed, and the meltdown spreads to every member of the household. This happens every day in countless homes across the country. We don't have control in our homes because we don't dispense authority to our children. There is a better way, as the principle of Gideon's ability to delegate shows.

As with Gideon's band of 300, you need to teach your children to act bigger than they are. If your child is six, empower him or her with responsibilities of an eight-year-old. Empower your fourteen-year-old to act seventeen. If you look back a hundred years or so, the average eight-year-old handled jobs and responsibilities that we don't even see teenagers taking on today. In our country today, we treat eight-year-olds as if they were six, and we treat seventeen-year-olds as if they were fourteen. Then we wonder why they can't accept responsibility, why they whine about people in authority, why they can't hold a job, why they can't pay their bills, why they need parental help as thirty-year-olds.

Do you see where I'm going here? Delegate responsibility to your children. Teach consequences. Nurture them and train them while you can.

Corporations fall victim to this tendency as well. I see so many managers who stay stressed out all the time because they have to do their employees' jobs for them. Why is that? It is a lack of effective delegation.

Rather than teaching well, then allowing the employees to grow into the job while accepting consequences for mistakes they make, managers keep walking on eggshells, doing whatever it takes to keep things running smoothly, fuming to themselves, "I'm apparently the only one that can do it right, so I gotta keep picking up the pieces and saving everyone else from utter destruction!"

Wrong! If you want to experience God's best—whether at home or at work—you can't do it all by yourself. You have to learn to dispense authority.

Be an example. Offer training. But at some point, delegate authority. Create a culture of effective delegation in your family, at your workplace, and in your ministry. Be willing to correct. If necessary, take back authority from people who can't (or won't) do the job.

Above all, honor those who do accept responsibility.

◾ Lessons in Delegation

So how can you learn to delegate?

Second Timothy teaches us how to delegate effectively: "You then, my son, be strong in the grace that is in Christ Jesus. And the things you have heard me say in the presence of many witnesses entrust to reliable men who will also be qualified to teach others" (2 Timothy 2:1–2).

I mentioned the four phases of leadership. Let's get more specific. In practical terms, delegation can be taught through these five simple steps:

RECRUIT

The way to attract the right person is found in verse one of the second letter from the Apostle Paul to the young Timothy. If you are strong in Christ, you will attract others with a similar quality. Light definitely attracts light. Leadership attracts leadership. Conversely, if you're sloppy, you will attract sloppy people.

> "What we love we shall grow to resemble."
>
> — BERNARD OF CLAIRVAUX

A single man who is overweight and out of shape may hope to attract an attractive woman, but he's more likely to attract someone like himself. As leadership expert John Maxwell says, "You don't attract who you want; you attract who you are." Whether you are filling a paying job or a volunteer position, you want the best person you can possibly get. Therefore, you need to be the best person you can possibly be.

If you are recruiting your family members at home, obviously you can't hire or fire your children; however, you can still model excellence in your life, which will inevitably rub off.

TRAIN

Sink or swim is a popular concept, but it seldom works. Before you can entrust others with responsibilities, you must first teach them. This building block is often neglected. Without the basic knowledge of the task a person is being asked to perform, he or she is likely to fail. It takes both on-the-job training and specialized training, where you have extra time to impart deeper understanding, such as in workshops or seminars.

MODEL

When training someone, model how you want something done first. This is the power of on-the-job training. People learn best by watching how someone else does something well. This is why, when Jesus wanted to raise up disciples, He did not just teach them—He had them live with Him so He could model a godly life. He knew that what they learned, day after day, would someday provide the foundation for reaching the known world with the Gospel.

COACH

Coaching means you let them do it as you make corrective adjustments while they work. Good coaching involves encouragement and honest feedback. Your children, employees, and team members need to always know how they are doing. The easy way out for any manager is to fume and fuss secretly, rather than confronting and offering proven, practical ways to do the job better. It takes effort. It takes tenacity. Yet nothing less will do if you want a powerful team.

While we are on the subject, coaching ideally involves pushing decisions as close as possible to the actual task. This should be obvious, but it is also very rare. How many times have you stood in line while the gum-smacking grocery-store cashier pages and repages a manager to come to the front to make a decision about a fifty-cent pack of whatever? Or how often have you sat on hold, listening to "Feelings" for the thirteenth time, while a customer service representative tries to track down a manager?

Empowering your people means educating and coaching them. But it also means giving them the freedom to make real-life decisions. After all, isn't that the point? Team members in a strong, flexible, growing organization must become very good at making decisions in the heat of battle, as Gideon's army did as they rolled through Oreb and Zeeb!

APPRECIATE

If you do not encourage people and appreciate them, they will get burned out and leave—it is as simple as that. We are all kids at heart, hardened around the edges and trying to function in the adult world, but still needing occasional "attaboys."

People need to know they are making a difference, and that their efforts are not going unnoticed. This may mean a simple pat on the back, a word of thanks, a thank-you card, a reward, a bonus for an employee, a gift certificate to a favorite restaurant, or simply allowing a child to stay up an hour later because he or she has been faithful about getting chores done with a great attitude.

One last principle of delegation that doesn't apply to everyone: If you are in a position of authority, there are times when you must be willing to fire someone. Call it whatever you want—termination, amicable parting of the ways, layoff, whatever—but if you are not willing to fire people who can't (or won't) perform, then you have no business hiring them.

You cannot enforce a standard of excellence unless you ultimately have the authority and the willingness to let people go when their performance is substandard. Even with volunteers, you must make the difficult decisions of moving people or providing another "opportunity" if they are deliberately or willingly hurting the cause.

Firing is always a last resort, done after retraining, coaching, and confrontations, but it becomes necessary at times if someone becomes unteachable, disloyal, or lacks the right attitude. This should be rare, and requires a heightened sensitivity and much prayer. Sometimes, however, it must be done, and you, dear leader, will have to do it for the good of the overall team.

How does this apply to you if you are not an employer or ministry leader? There may be occasions when you have asked someone to help you with something but later find that the person isn't working out. You may need to find a way to gently let that person off the hook and say that you won't need his or her help any longer. In some ways, this can be more difficult than the task an employer faces when firing someone. In one case, it's an employer-employee relationship; in the other, a friendship may be at stake. This is a time when you need to seek God's wisdom and guidance as to how to move forward.

> "The desire to be appreciated is one of the deepest drives in human nature."
> — WILLIAM JAMES

The best way to avoid such a situation is to be careful in who you ask to be on your team. Make sure that you are enlisting the help of people whom you know you can count on, and who can count on you. Delegation can and should be rewarding for everyone involved as you build a powerful team based on trust, integrity, hard work, and fun.

To reach your goals, you must learn to delegate. Gideon did, and the results were nothing short of spectacular for him, his army, and his nation.

Looking Back–Looking Forward

Gideon modeled many admirable things. He and his men learned to set goals, to act bigger than they really were, to stay humble even in the midst of a rout, to rely upon others through delegation, and to finish the job—moving from victory to victory!

What we should learn from this is that life rewards action, not intentions.

There were many points of no return for Gideon and his army. At each point, even up to the moment before Gideon raised his trumpet to his mouth and took a powerful, tension-filled breath, he could have said, "Wait a minute, here! Let's think things through. Do we really want to toot our horns and break pottery right now? We might wake up that huge army of mean guys who are sleeping out there. Let's have a task force and think through all the alternatives."

No. When the moment of truth arrived, Gideon showed true leadership by pulling the proverbial trigger. At Oreb and Zeeb, Gideon's soldiers showed the same fortitude. Decisive action, not mere intention, wins wars on any field of endeavor.

Dwight L. Moody, one of America's greatest ministers, once asked one of his associates about a task that needed to be done. The worker said, "We've been aimin' to do that for almost a year, but we just haven't got around to it."

Moody replied, "Do you think it's about time to stop aiming and start firing?"

Too many people get caught up in the "Ready, aim, aim, aim . . ." syndrome. They are always planning but never taking action.

Why? Inaction usually results from:

- The fear of failing

- A terminal case of "Someday, I'll . . ."

- Preferring busy-ness instead of business

- No workable, inspired plan of action

I love the Nike slogan that has been around for years: "Just do it!" That ad campaign, in one form or another, has lasted decades because it goes to the core of success in athletics and life.

It is not enough to just stay busy. Many hard-working, busy-looking people are anything but successful. At some point it becomes vital to act, to actually begin taking the steps that will fulfill the vision God has given you.

You may fail.

I have, many times. But the only way to keep from making mistakes or risking failure is to do absolutely nothing, and that, in the end, is the gravest error of all.

Failure is not always bad. In fact, Thomas J. Watson Sr., the founder of IBM, once said, "The way to succeed is to double your failure rate."

Likewise, one of Thomas Edison's assistants complained one day, "Mr. Edison, we have tried five hundred experiments to find a solution to this problem, but we still haven't had any results." The prolific American inventor smiled and replied, "My friend, we do have results. We now know five hundred ways that will not work!"

A failure is only a loss when you learn nothing from the experience, and it is only a disaster when you let it defeat you.

Plans only have power when you execute them. The secret of overcoming inaction is to learn to push aside what seems urgent at the moment and, with God's help, to concentrate on what is important for the long run.

Actions really do speak louder than words. Learning how to act decisively is a powerful step toward learning to seek nothing less than God's best.

ACTION PLAN

? Spend a few minutes in prayer, thanking God for how He has worked in your life and asking for wisdom to act decisively on the plan you have been developing. If you need some help in further clarifying your long-range goals, go beyond five-year goals, even if only for the sake of stretching your imagination. Complete the following sentences. Read through them, and then take out your notebook and jot down the first thing that pops into your mind for each one.

1. My greatest priorities in life are:

2. My best talents, personally and professionally, are:

3. My life is:

4. Ten years from now, I will probably live (where?):

5. Ten years from now, I will likely be doing:

6. Ten years from now, I will likely own assets of:

7. Ten years from now, I will be happy because:

8. More than anything, I want:

Take a few moments to reflect on your answers. What do your sentences say about your hopes for the future?

When you think through your projections for the future, you begin to discover what controls your approach toward life. Once you understand what is affecting your attitude about life itself, you will uncover the forces and attitudes that are already impacting your future.

GIDEON and his three hundred men, exhausted yet keeping up the pursuit, came to the Jordan and crossed it.

(JUDGES 8:4)

STEP NINE

FACE CHALLENGES HEAD-ON

Learning how to change, follow God's call, and seek His best is a process. As Gideon learned, God desires to give you a vision, to help you develop a plan of action, and to direct your steps as you achieve more.

No matter where you are in life right now, the opportunity to experience an abundance of God's blessings in your life is very real, but so is the struggle to handle the blessings. Maintaining your success is often more difficult than the initial struggle. Anytime you accomplish something worthwhile, there are always new challenges, and the key to success is in facing them head-on.

Let's recap: Gideon and his army witnessed a certified miracle at daybreak as the Midianite army and eastern tribesmen self-destructed in the face of trumpets, torches in just-broken clay pots, and shouts of, "A sword for the LORD and for Gideon!"

The rout turned into a marathon as the enemy ran for home and a growing number of Israel's men joined the pursuit. Victory after victory followed, including historic triumphs over the Midianite princes Oreb and Zeeb.

But the victory was incomplete. There was still much to be done. At this moment in Gideon's life, he would be tested with one of the ultimate challenges that make or break champions. He had to learn the painful lessons that inevitably come with success.

Success is not a one-shot deal. One of the toughest parts of achievement is maintaining success. You might have an incredible marriage, but the hard part is nurturing it over a lifetime. Maybe you have a great career, but can you be successful and still stay balanced in every area of life? Perhaps you have a huge, powerful ministry, but can you maintain that level of success over the long haul?

The issue is not just winning a victory. The hard part is also about sustaining success. There are so many distractions but so few encouragers, so little time and so many obstacles that come against you when you begin to achieve. Add to that the tendency many of us have to self-destruct, and even in success you can find a blueprint for failure.

But people who experience God's best on a continuing basis are people who have learned to face whatever challenges and obstacles come their way.

Sadly, those challenges often start with those who are closest to you.

■ The Challenge of Criticism

The tendency to criticize is part of human nature, I suppose. People love to kick others when they fail, but they really, *really* enjoy knocking others when they succeed. It is a fact of life, and the sooner you accept it, the better you will be able to handle success.

"If what they are saying about you is true, mend your ways. If it isn't true, forget it, and go on and serve the Lord."

— HARRY A. IRONSIDE

If you don't believe it, the next time you run into the neighborhood grocery store, take a look at the front pages of all the tabloids at the checkout lanes. How much ink is used every week to taunt those in the public eye who fail and to spew jealous disdain on those who succeed? Without those two extremes, print tabloids, online gossip sites, and broadcast celebrity shows would go out of business tomorrow.

At least Gideon didn't have to worry about the paparazzi when he and his band of 300 defeated the Midianites and eastern tribesmen. What he did have to contend with, almost immediately, were cheap shots from his own countrymen.

Gideon was exhausted. He and his men had routed most of the Midianite army, but the victory was still not complete. The remaining Midianites began to run. In the process of chasing down the leftover enemy soldiers, he ran headlong into his own neighbors and family members. And they were not happy: "Now the Ephraimites asked Gideon, 'Why have you treated us like this? Why didn't you call us when you went to fight Midian?' And they criticized him sharply" (Judges 8:1).

Unfortunately, maintaining success means dealing with criticism. If you are not being criticized, then you are probably not attempting anything beyond the norm. However, when you begin to step out with God, taking new risks, accomplishing beyond mediocrity, and heading toward excellence, others around you will begin to criticize you. When you begin to experience God's best, criticism will become an everyday, normal event.

You need to get used to criticism; you also need to learn how to handle it.

Let's look at how Gideon handled criticism: "But he answered them, 'What have I accomplished compared to you? Aren't the gleanings of Ephraim's grapes better than the full grape harvest of Abiezer?'" (Judges 8:2).

Abiezer is Gideon's clan. In essence, Gideon said, "I can't touch what you've accomplished." It was a wise response to criticism. He didn't whine. He didn't attack. He just reminded the Ephraimites what God had

> "A thick skin is a gift from God."
>
> — KONRAD ADENAUER

done and then said, "God gave Oreb and Zeeb, the Midianite leaders, into your hands. What was I able to do compared to you?"

It takes two parties to fight. Gideon had already proved his courage on the battlefield. He also knew that the worst thing he could do was start battling his own countrymen, thereby ensuring self-destruction and thwarting total victory.

What happened?

The same thing happened that takes place most of the time when you handle' a potentially explosive situation correctly. At this, the Ephraimites' resentment against Gideon subsided.

Gideon was a genius. When people criticized him, he did not respond in kind. He did not answer their criticism with criticism.

Yes, he could have blasted back at his critics and told them to shove off. Israel had not changed a thing after all those years of oppression, until Gideon stood up and with God's power took steps to make a difference. But even though Gideon's response would have been justified, he knew that arguing wouldn't accomplish anything.

> Answering your critics only wastes your time and makes you play into their hands.

Gideon wisely recognized that there was nothing good that could come from arguing with someone who is criticizing you, especially when it's someone close to you.

There is a lesson here that we should not gloss over. When someone surpasses us in any area, our natural, selfish human tendency is to attack him or her. When I'm driving in my car on the highway there could be no one around me for miles, but the moment I see a car off in the distance, I've gotta pass it.

Men, you know what I'm talking about, don't you? There's just something built in us that makes us uncomfortable with people passing us or being in front of us. And people are not comfortable if you have surpassed them in any way. Excelling is a natural way to get criticism.

Someone once said, "If you stick your head above the crowd, expect to get hit with a few ripe tomatoes."

Gideon's success drew criticism. So what? When he was attacked by one of his own clan, Gideon did not turn around and deny his success. He did not deny what God had done in his life. That would be to deny the supernatural miracles God had performed.

What Gideon did, rather, was to point out all that the Ephraimites had accomplished. When he did that, the criticism subsided. He said, "Wait a minute. Look what you guys have accomplished. Look at all the stuff you've done."

How do you answer criticism? You make the other person feel important.

Value other people by pointing out all they have accomplished, even if it pales in comparison to what you have done. Find the good in what they have achieved.

I'm just telling you the simple truth of the matter. It's the wisdom of Jesus—turn the other cheek. The best way to solve your problem with an enemy is to make them a friend. The way you do that is by pointing out the good that they have accomplished and what they have been able to do.

The world-class leaders that I have met—every single one of them—never seem to want to talk about themselves. Isn't that amazing? Those whom I have met kept asking me questions about what I did, my family, my ministry, and other topics that paled in comparison to their accomplishments. Wow! That has left an indelible impression on me.

As you learn to seek God's best, sustain your victories by taking a hint from Gideon and those who understand true success. Focus on others. Ask about what is going on in their lives. Seek to find out what God is doing through them.

As you become more and more successful, just sharing your time with others is a great way to sustain your achievement. It is another way to make others feel important. Showing genuine interest in those around you not only keeps you in touch and human but also lets you keep your ear to the ground, so to speak. In other words, it keeps you connected with your team, their feelings, their struggles, and their needs. Step into their world, show them honor, build rapport. Take the time to notice the

> The number one subject that people want to talk about is themselves.

> "The stones the critics hurl with harsh intent, a man may use to build his monument."
>
> — ARTHUR GUTTERMAN

contributions they make every day. By doing this, you will defuse much criticism before it ever starts.

One way I do this on occasion is to go by someone's office or place of work and ask for a tour. You can see firsthand what they do, and they feel honored that you care enough to take the time to notice the contribution they make day to day. Let people brag on what they do.

It needs to be genuine interest or it will backfire. People are cynical today and can smell a con job a mile away. If you can't be genuine, then don't do it.

Apparently Gideon came through as genuine. He reflected the interest. He defused the problem. When you make other people feel important, then you are no longer a threat to them. I'm telling you, this works time and again.

The next time someone criticizes you, take the following steps to handle the situation and sustain your success:

LOOK FOR THE KERNEL OF TRUTH IN CRITICISM AND MAKE APPROPRIATE CHANGES

Often there is a partial truth to be found in criticism. We can learn a lot from critics. Never ignore truth about yourself just because it is painful. If you listen to your critics, you can improve drastically. Plus, if people are criticizing you out of jealousy, nothing will frustrate them more than for you to shore up your weaknesses.

IF THERE IS NO REDEMPTIVE NATURE TO WHAT SOMEONE IS SAYING, IGNORE IT

Sometimes people are just plain negative or mean-spirited. This is the kind of criticism that says a lot more about the one offering it than about the person being criticized.

If others are spreading lies, of course, you may need to confront them. However, if it is just negative or subjective opinion, disregard what they are saying and don't worry about it.

I know this is easier to write than to live out. Once when I was being heavily criticized, I called a mentor of mine, Scott Weatherford (an amazing leader of leaders). A family had left our ministry and they were saying very negative things that were completely false. Scott asked me if what they were saying was true. I told him there was no truth to it whatsoever. Then he asked me if it hurt that they were leaving. I was a little surprised.

"Of course it hurts," I replied.

Then Scott said something that only a great leader could say because he had already lived through many similar situations. Scott told me, "Bil, I'd be more worried if it didn't hurt, because then you would no longer be a lover of people."

It is okay to be hurt. Just don't live life as a constant response to people who are negative.

IF GOD LEADS YOU TO DO SO, CALL THE PEOPLE CRITICIZING YOU

Sometimes it's not a bad idea to contact the people who are criticizing you and let them vent. Let them know you have heard their grievances and that you intend to address them. In a way, this is what Gideon did with his fellow Ephraimites.

However, I make this suggestion with a warning. If you follow up every criticism made about you and try to confront the ones making it, you won't have time to do what God wants you to do. In other words, criticism can distract you from the task God has called you to. If there is enough criticism going on about an issue, you are probably a leader stepping out in faith and don't need to change a thing.

Why do we have this tendency to criticize others? Remember the prettiest girl back in high school? Everyone loved her, at least to her face. Behind her back, however, she was often the most criticized. People called her ugly. Some of the girls in school would say, "Oh, look at her. Can you believe that dress she's wearing? She looks terrible. I can't believe she wore that eye shadow. I can't believe it." All the criticism was based on jealousy. And we need to keep in mind that we can also be tempted to criticize others when we think they're more successful than we are.

The truth is, someone else's success doesn't have to detract from your success, and vice versa. There is plenty of success to go around. There is no scarcity with God. We have a God of abundance and a God who has put an entire universe at our disposal. If others have a bigger piece of the pie, or even if it seems they have the entire pie, so to speak, there is no need to worry. God is still making more pie.

Instead we should follow the instructions Paul gave in Romans: "Rejoice with those who rejoice; mourn with those who mourn" (Romans 12:15). It is okay to rejoice when things go well with others. And it is okay to mourn with them as well. When people criticize you, often the barbs come because of things going on in their lives. Your success may seem like an open wound to them in comparison to what they are experiencing at that moment. And you don't even know what other struggles they are experiencing. Everyone has different blessings and different seasons of blessing.

With success comes criticism. When you are doing something significant, you will attract criticism. If you cannot handle being criticized, you will be susceptible to being emotionally manipulated by your critics.

> "If people speak ill of you, live so that no one will believe them."
>
> — PLATO

Just remember what Gideon did with the Ephraimites. He knew that the Lord had given the victories. He knew who should get the glory. When others criticized him, Gideon rested on a firm foundation.

What is necessary for you to maintain success in the face of criticism? Humility and the understanding that God should get all the glory.

The Challenge of Exhaustion

In Judges 8:4 we see another challenge to sustained success: exhaustion. "Gideon and his 300 men, exhausted yet keeping up the pursuit, came to the Jordan and crossed it."

Exhaustion implies hard work. Gideon handled criticism well, despite being worn out. However, exhaustion itself could have become a great obstacle to his sustained effectiveness.

For God to bless you in a great way, you are going to have to work hard. There is no getting around that. A lot of times, however, people believe that when God moves mightily in their lives, everything will be a breeze. God will help you delegate, right? God will give you great strength, right? God will make sure you catch your proverbial second wind, right?

Not always. Success breeds success, of course, but great achievement often means that you will have to work harder than ever before.

Those whom God finds faithful usually get even more to do. We see it in the parable of the talents in the New Testament. We see it in the lives of people throughout the Bible. We see it today.

When you pray, "God, bless me with more," get ready. Be careful what you pray for, because you may get it. And when you get more, more will be expected. That is a faith-filled fact of life.

Maybe it is better to pray, "First of all, God, help me to handle what I'm currently doing better, so that I'll be ready for more when You give it." You cannot ask for God to dump more on your plate until you first ask God to increase the size of your plate—your capacity to handle more. Ask God to increase your capacity to handle His blessing.

The Challenge of False Friends

Even though Gideon and his men were exhausted, they made the choice to keep on keeping on, to "not become weary in doing good," knowing that "at the proper time we will reap a harvest if we do not give up" (Galatians 6:9). Granted, Paul's letter to the church in Galatia was not written until centuries after Gideon was dead and gone, but the principle is one that runs throughout God's Word!

Even though they were worn out, Gideon and his 300 men crossed the Jordan River. When they reached Succoth they were tired, hungry, and needed a break. Gideon asked the leaders of the town, "Please give my warriors some food. They are very tired. I am chasing Zebah and Zalmunna, the kings of Midian" (Judges 8:5, NLT).

The question was very simple: "Hey, my guys are worn out. Can you give them some grub so we can keep ridding the countryside of the bad guys?"

In Judges 8:6, the leaders of Succoth replied, "Do you already have the hands of Zebah and Zalmunna in your possession? Why should we give bread to your troops?" In other words, "You haven't caught the bad guys yet. Catch them first, and then we will think about feeding your warriors." Nice guys, right?

> "Well done is better than well said."
> — BENJAMIN FRANKLIN

Gideon's reply was right to the point: "After the LORD gives me victory over Zebah and Zalmunna, I will return and tear your flesh with the thorns and briers from the wilderness" (Judges 8:7, NLT).

In our era of political correctness, it is important for us to remember that all of the Scripture is inspired—even the portions that are more difficult with which to deal.

At that moment, food meant the difference between life and death, between ultimate victory and miserable defeat. The last thing Gideon's army needed was to have to stop, gather food, and prepare meals, meanwhile allowing the Midianites and eastern tribesmen to regroup, reinforce, and return.

The leaders of Succoth picked a bad time to mess with Gideon. He was tired. He was agitated. The victories thus far had liberated the land of terrorists and thugs. All he wanted was a little food for his men. "No!" was not the correct answer. Neither was "Later!" Later would probably have been too late. In the midst of war, denial of help is choosing a side. The leaders of Succoth didn't just refuse to give food to Gideon's men; their refusal aided the enemy.

And if that was not bad enough, look at what happened next: "From there he went up to Peniel and made the same request of them, but they answered as the men of Succoth had. So he said to the men of Peniel, 'When I return in triumph, I will tear down this tower'" (Judges 8:8–9).

Perhaps it was merely human nature for the men of Succoth and Peniel to step back, refuse to choose sides, and wait to see who won. As soon as Gideon was declared a winner, then they could sidle up to him and boast, "You're the man, Gideon. We were with you all along." They were "Succothing" up to whoever would win in the end. They did not want to get involved. For many people, this becomes their excuse in life.

You knew these people in elementary school, you knew them in high school, you have met them in the workplace, and you will meet up with these people at every step of your life.

Gideon's rebuke was understandable, especially when you consider the fact that he was in the midst of war. It is no wonder he said, "You know what, guys? This isn't going to fly with me. I am fighting a war for the protection and the freedom of everyone, including you. And if you don't support it, then you will pay for it. I don't have the time or energy to mess with you now, but there will be consequences later."

Gideon was apparently not angry for himself. He was understand-ably angry because he had seen his men wounded and tired. We don't even know how many of his men, at that point, were lying dead on the battlefield. He had to be thinking, "I just watched men that I love give everything for you people here in Succoth and Peniel. I know their families, and their children are not going to have a dad now. Some of the wives aren't going to have husbands anymore. These soldiers who are with me represent the finest in our country. They have fought for your freedom. And now you have the audacity to say, 'I dunno. I think

I'm going to hold back water and bread until I see what happens. You never know who might win this.'"

At that moment, Gideon is righteously angry. As we say in Texas, "He ain't messin' 'round!" Gideon let the people of Succoth and Peniel know, in no uncertain terms, that what they did was treason. By withholding food, they were helping the enemy.

> "A real friend is one who walks in when the rest of the world walks out."
>
> — WALTER WINCHELL

Granted, you're probably not reading this book in order to plan a military conquest. Nevertheless, what happened to Gideon here contains an important lesson to learn for those who want to find God's will for their lives. I really believe that sometimes God will permit struggles in your life just so you can see who your real friends are, so you can know whom you can really trust.

You can learn several lessons from this incident that will help sustain your success.

LEARN THE DIFFERENCE BETWEEN FRIENDS AND MIGHT-BE FRIENDS

Sometimes God uses challenges so you can see who is standing with you and who is walking away. When life is falling apart, it is important to know that the person you call at 3:00 AM will answer the phone, listen to you, help you, and stay close.

When you call needing help, counsel, money, a kind word, you don't need to hear, "Gee, I dunno. I'm kind of busy right now. Maybe later."

When things are falling apart, when life is messy, when you are in the midst of battle, your true friends will shine. Those who hesitate or walk away are not your friends. Learning the contrast between true friends and fair-weather acquaintances can make the difference between life and death at critical times in your life.

Learning this principle can also mean the difference between being a one-time wonder and a long-term champion.

Gideon confronts the men of Peniel and Succoth and lets them know in no uncertain terms that they did not support him when he needed it most, so when the victory comes, they will not share in the celebration.

LEARN THAT PEOPLE RARELY TURN THEIR BACKS ON YOU AT CONVENIENT TIMES

It would be nice if you could learn the hard lessons while sipping lemonade beside a swimming pool as you count stacks of money and your family stands by with hushed reverence.

It doesn't work like that. Fair-weather people will become unsupportive at precisely the worst moments, right when you are tired, hassled, broke, and facing horrible deadlines. That makes it all the more important that when you are building your team, you surround yourself with people who are true friends, people you know you can count on during the tough times.

LEARN TO TRUST, BUT VERIFY

One of my mentors taught me that when people who have turned on you come back into your life, as they sometimes will, it is healthy to keep your guard up.

"Trust but verify," first attributed to fiction writer Damon Runyon, was a signature phrase of President Ronald Reagan. When he used this phrase, he was usually discussing relations with the Soviet Union and he almost always presented it as a translation of the Russian proverb "*doveriai, no proveriai*." At the signing of the INF Treaty to reduce nuclear weapons, he used it again, and his Soviet counterpart, Mikhail Gorbachev, responded: "You repeat this phrase every time we meet." The more we learn about that era, the more sense the phrase makes.

"Trust but verify" doesn't mean that we always go around harboring grudges or that we're perpetually distrustful of others. It just means that we should take seriously another proverb: "Fool me once, shame on you. Fool me twice, shame on me."

My mentor Scott also told me, "Don't close your heart off to people, but sometimes you simply have to be wise in your relationships if you are going to be able to sustain success. You have to realize that there are toxic people who knowingly or unknowingly design their lives around who they can use next."

When people who have dropped the ball or walked out on you in the past want to be restored to your team, it's okay to bring them back. But you also need to be wise and cautious—to "trust but verify"—in your dealings with them.

LEARN TO BUILD SUSTAINABLE RELATIONSHIPS

My wife loves me, not because my ministry is going good or bad, but simply because she loves me. I love her because I love her, not because of anything good or bad that might be happening in her life at any given point. That is a sustainable relationship.

Bill Hybels, pastor of Willow Creek Community Church, says that every relationship that you have with other people is like an ATM machine. Every time you have an interaction with others, they are either making a withdrawal or a deposit. If you have people around you who only want to make withdrawals, you cannot sustain those friendships.

Look instead for people who strive to make an equal amount of deposits and withdrawals from you. Those relationships will be keepers, sustainable ones.

Then, when you are down, they will be there to build you up. When you are up, you will have something positive to pour into their lives. It has to go both ways.

People who are "depositors" light you up. They encourage you. They build you. They understand, even when the tough times come, that cutting and running are not options.

The men of Succoth were only interested in befriending the winner of the battle, for their own needs and security to be taken care of. They were "Succothing" up and Gideon knew it.

To maintain success in your life, you need a number of strong friendships and relationships. As Gideon learned, it was the only way he could complete what God had set out for him to do.

We don't know how Gideon and his men were able to keep going. All we do know is that they completed the job.

The Challenge of Finishing

Judges 8:11–12 tells us, "Gideon went up by the route of the nomads east of Nobah and Jogbehah and fell upon the unsuspecting army. Zebah and Zalmunna, the two kings of Midian, fled, but he pursued them and captured them, routing their entire army."

"Entire" is an awfully large term. Quite simply, it means that at daybreak on the day of trumpets and torches, Gideon's band of 300 stealthily surrounded 135,000 Midianites and eastern tribesmen. By the end of the campaign the enemy had been routed.

> "The best mirror is an old friend."
>
> — GEORGE HERBERT

We don't know how many days it took—perhaps two, three, or even a week—but we do know that God's Word doesn't leave any interpretation or wiggle room about the results. Gideon pursued them, captured them, and routed the entire army. Period. End of story.

Okay, it is not the "end of the story" (as we will discuss in the remainder of this chapter and the final step), but that phrase is meant to add an exclamation point to the fact that Gideon was a finisher.

Gideon finished the battle. And he even finished by returning to Succoth and Peniel to take care of business there: "Gideon son of Joash then returned from the battle by the Pass of Heres. He caught a young man of Succoth and questioned him, and the young man wrote down for him the names of the seventy-seven officials of Succoth, the elders of the town" (Judges 8:13–14).

> "Do not plan for ventures before finishing what's at hand."
>
> — EURIPIDES

You can't improve on the script of what happened. Gideon grabbed a young man: "Where are you from?"

"Succoth."

"Oh really. Could you list off the names of all the elders of your town for me?"

"Where is the pencil and paper?"

Maybe Gideon intimidated this young man by saying something like this: "Succoth Boy, it's either the names or your life!" Possibly, Gideon's reputation had preceded him so that he just had to say, "Give me the names."

Either way, he got the names of the town elders. In those days it was common for people to be able list off every elder of their city. Their government officials didn't rotate and have term limits like we have in modern Western societies. If you became an elder in that day, you were an elder till you died. The word *elder*, by the way, means "leader." So if you were a leader in the community, you were a leader for the rest of your life.

Finishers like Gideon understand personal responsibility, so they hold people accountable. This is why Gideon took down every single name.

Next, Gideon heads over to Succoth and says, "Hey, guys! I'm back!"

Quickly the town leaders got a thrashing with desert thorns and briars. Obviously, I have never personally been beaten like that, but it doesn't sound like fun.

While this may seem harsh to us, keep in mind that Gideon was dealing with life-and-death situations. He wanted to make sure that if he and his warriors ever faced a similar situation and showed up in Succoth again, that history wouldn't repeat itself. His bite was much louder than his bark. He delivered what he promised.

Gideon also punished the men of Peniel who refused to feed his soldiers during the pursuit. "He also pulled down the tower of Peniel and killed the men of the town" (Judges 8:17).

Gideon delivered more than he promised to the two Midianite kings Zebah and Zalmunna, who he discovered had killed his own brothers. In short order, Gideon had a gladiator moment, avenged his siblings' deaths, and even took the ornaments off the victims' camels' necks, according to verse 21.

It is not a pretty sight, but Gideon was a finisher. He was sending a clear signal to all the surrounding nations that Israel would not be intimidated. He finished what he started. His acts helped guarantee peace in a land that had known little peace.

This may all seem a bit grisly, but keep in mind that I'm not saying that we should go out and thrash people who don't help us. And I'm obviously not saying we should be killing our enemies. The point is that Gideon sustained his victory by finishing what he started. The lesson is clear for us as well.

You will not maintain your success in life, let alone get there, if you do not become a good finisher. Many people are good at starting things, but only a few finish what they start. Inspiration will get you started, but it takes perspiration to finish. The price of sustained success is high.

Few people are willing to pay that price.

The Challenge of Wealth

Gideon faced many challenges following his great victory over Midian. But perhaps the greatest was the temptation to seize wealth and power. Gideon never mentioned money in any of his negotiations with God or his fellow men. Not once during the requests for signs did Gideon ever say, "Oh, by the way, God, can You also dump out a mountain of gold while You are at it?" And not once did he go to his countrymen prior to the battle and say anything like this: "Oh, get out your pocketbooks. I don't work cheaply. I need a ton of your money before I commit to taking on the Midianites, and then I'll need another ton when I complete the job."

Regardless, when the job was over, people far and wide were willing to reward Gideon for a job well done. We read this in Judges 8:22–23:

> The Israelites said to Gideon, "Rule over us—you, your son and your grandson—because you have saved us out of the hand of Midian." But Gideon told them, "I will not rule over you, nor will my son rule over you. The LORD will rule over you."

As a supreme ruler, Gideon could have taken anything he wanted from the land. But Gideon did not want power. He wanted freedom. He wanted to be rid of the intimidation, oppression, and terrorism that had plagued the land for years. Gideon fought with the vision of being free to do whatever God wanted him to do—nothing more, nothing less. His goal was to win back his freedom for his family, his community, and ultimately, his country.

Yet while he didn't crave power, Gideon understood these principles that run throughout Scripture: "Do not muzzle the ox while it is treading out the grain," and "The worker deserves his wages" (1 Timothy 5:18).

Gideon had been willing to commit his life for the nation of Israel, no matter what it cost him or his family. He had been willing to put everything on the line. His answer shows that he was wise about life and the secret of true wealth:

> And he said, "I do have one request, that each of you give me an earring from your share of the plunder." (It was the custom of the Ishmaelites to wear gold earrings.) They answered, "We'll

be glad to give them." So they spread out a garment, and each man threw a ring from his plunder onto it. The weight of the gold rings he asked for came to seventeen hundred shekels, not counting the ornaments, the pendants and the purple garments worn by the kings of Midian or the chains that were on their camels' necks. (Judges 8:24–26)

As was the custom of war back then, the men took home what riches they could carry in order to begin life anew after the war. Gideon apparently did not take any of the plunder. Instead, Gideon decided to ask for a percentage of the gross profits of Israel's victory. This was a very smart move on his behalf, because his pay, though large, cost each giver relatively little. He was wise, but he definitely wasn't greedy. Each of the soldiers took home a lot, and they were more than willing to share a little of their reward with their leader. As a result, Gideon set up his family financially for a very long time without costing Israel much at all.

Gideon taught a powerful secret of wealth building. One of the secrets to long-term wealth building is to take a small percentage from a large amount, to not be greedy, to not seek get-rich-quick schemes. The power was in the multiple. Gideon did not want a lot from one transaction; he wanted a little from a lot of transactions. This is taking what you do to a multiple.

Most people want a large percentage from one sale, yet the big payoffs rarely happen. That is why it is much smarter, if you're a salesperson, to seek a smaller percentage and increase your sales. I have heard it expressed this way—"Sell to the classes and you'll live with the masses, but sell to the masses and you'll live with the classes." A lot of little or nothing usually ends up being little or nothing. A little of a lot equals a lot, no matter what the percentages are.

It stands to reason that Gideon should have been paid for his service to Israel. Likewise, there is nothing wrong with building wealth and earning a good living. In fact, there is more wrong with not earning a good living—it hurts your family, it potentially hurts your children's ability to further their education, and if financial struggles persist, it has been proven to become a real barrier to healthy marriages.

> "Money is power, freedom, a cushion, the root of all evil, the sum of blessings."
>
> — CARL SANDBURG

Gideon paid a dear price for what he received. He could have easily ended up on the wrong end of a Midianite sword. Instead, God used him to help pull off one of history's greatest military victories. Gideon's huge risks paid off handsomely for Israel, and in return, for himself.

Following Gideon's example, there are lessons you can learn for building wealth while avoiding the temptation of greed.

DECIDE TO CHANGE

When you get sick and tired of being sick and tired, you have reached the point when you are willing to change whatever is required to get moving in a new direction. The definition of insanity, I have heard, is doing the same old thing over and over, yet continually expecting a different result or outcome.

Unless you are willing to change, nothing changes.

In Gideon's case, his desire was to stop putting up with intimidation from the Midianite bullies and eastern tribe marauders. He was sick and tired of having his crops stolen. He was sick and tired of having to hide out in the valley winepress in order to glean a little grain for his family to eat. When God gave a new vision, he was ready to do whatever it took to change the way things were.

If you are ready to change, ask God for a new vision. He may give you an inventive idea for your own business. He may lead you into real estate. He may give you favor in a revolutionary intellectual property. He may guide you into investments. There are thousands of opportunities that are available to help you create a strategy to build wealth.

APPLY THE MULTIPLICATION PRINCIPLE

Multiply what you already know. If your house is worth more today than it was five years ago because of appreciation, why not own ten houses and multiply that appreciation?

What skills and talents do you have? Teach a seminar about what you know, multiplying your knowledge into dozens, perhaps hundreds or thousands of other lives. Or write a book about what you know and see if it can be delivered to a mass audience. Start a business on the side selling a worthwhile product that you use personally and can market professionally.

There are many ways to use the creativity God gave you to multiply what you know and build into the lives of others.

STOP "APPROACH AVOIDANCE" WHEN IT COMES TO WEALTH

You have heard the old phrase, "Don't shoot yourself in the foot." I am not sure where the phrase started, but it couldn't have been from a good experience.

Today, this happens when people are at the cusp of earning a lot of money. Then they start feeling guilty and they begin self-destructing, backing off from the big pay-days. Better you should follow the principle offered in Psalm 62:10: "Though your riches increase, do not set your heart on them."

> "Money isn't the most important thing in life, but it's reasonably close to oxygen on the 'gotta have it' scale."
>
> — ZIG ZIGLAR

When the payoff came for Gideon, he knew that everything about the victories he had experienced had been miraculous. The golden bonus was just another in a long string of miracles, and he didn't hold back from whatever God was setting up for the future.

WHEN THE PAYOFFS COME, ADJUST YOUR LIFESTYLE SLOWLY

The concept of *nouveau riche* (the French term for "new rich") refers to people with newfound wealth who lack the experience, taste, and wisdom to use wealth wisely; typically they come from a lower class of society, spend their newfound money quickly and conspicuously, and then return penniless to the lower-class life with nothing to show for what they had.

A fool and his money are soon parted. Don't be foolish. Adjust your lifestyle slowly. Set aside money from everything you make for the future. Make wise investments. Keep planting seed. Enjoy the harvest, but not too much.

NEVER MAKE MONEY INTO YOUR GOD

On this point, Gideon failed miserably, as we will see in the next chapter.

> "Money is like manure; it's not worth a thing unless it's spread around encouraging young things to grow."
> — THORNTON WILDER, *THE MATCHMAKER*

Ecclesiastes 5:10 tells us, "Whoever loves money never has money enough; whoever loves wealth is never satisfied with his income."

The purpose of wealth is to do something worthwhile with it, to build the local church, to help take the Gospel around the globe, to impact your generation, and to share your wealth-building principles with others. Anything less is folly and vanity.

Give glory to God for all He has done. Bring your tithe to God's house, no matter what your income level, whether a little or a lot. Then watch God fulfill the words of the prophet Malachi:

> "Bring the whole tithe into the storehouse, that there may be food in my house. Test me in this," says the LORD Almighty, "and see if I will not throw open the floodgates of heaven and pour out so much blessing that you will not have room enough for it. I will prevent pests from devouring your crops, and the vines in your fields will not cast their fruit," says the LORD Almighty. "Then all the nations will call you blessed,

for yours will be a delightful land," says the LORD Almighty. (Malachi 3:10–12)

Now that's what I call seeking nothing less than God's best!

Looking Back–Looking Forward

Nobody wins every skirmish or goes through life unscathed or un-criticized. If you cannot conquer every foe, the secret is to decide which victories are worth fighting for and which are not. As you attempt to climb higher in life, there are two ways you can view obstacles.

OBSTACLES CAN STRENGTHEN YOU OR DESTROY YOU

When you misunderstand the purpose of struggles and allow them to breed discouragement, you de-energize the benefits.

As Gideon discovered, there comes a time in every person's life when every resource you have is tested, when life seems unfair, when your faith and courage and power to persist are pushed to the limits and beyond.

Some people see these tests as excuses to quit, to give up, to let someone else do what must be done. Others, like Gideon, use these tests as opportunities to propel them toward greater success and victories.

OBSTACLES OFFER AN OPPORTUNITY TO MEASURE YOUR GROWTH

Challenges come to help you see how far you have come. Look upon each problem as another chance to measure how much more strength, faith, and courage you have.

Difficulties, criticisms, pain, and disappointment can actually ac-celerate your development, especially when you understand the value of each. For in the midst of those challenges, you learn the value of faith and persistence.

President Calvin Coolidge wrote: "Nothing in the world can take the place of persistence. Talent will not; nothing is more common than unsuccessful men with talent. Genius will not; unrewarded genius is almost a proverb. Education will not; the world is full of educated derelicts. Persistence and determination alone are omnipotent."

Persistence is a conscious decision to finish the job, no matter what happens. It is a bulldog-like choice to complete the task, regardless of the criticism or changes you face. And the rewards for godly persistence are unlimited—in this life and the next.

Finish whatever you start and see what happens when you make persistence a way of life. The change you seek will come. God's best will come.

ACTION PLAN

? The difference between success and failure is often found in a person's attitudes toward criticism, defeats, mistakes, and other setbacks. After you've spent some time in prayer, talking to God about the challenges you face, take out your notebook, and write down your answers to the following questions:

1. What is the worst criticism you have received in the past?

2. What did you learn from that criticism?

3. Do you have the courage to be your own constructive critic? In what ways?

4. What are the best ways you have been able to overcome discouragement?

5. What skill, talent, ability, or interest do you have that you could multiply into the lives of others?

6. How will you begin to multiply that talent this week?

GIDEON made the gold into an ephod, which he placed in Ophrah, his town. All Israel prostituted themselves by worshiping it there, and it became a snare to Gideon and his family. Thus Midian was subdued before the Israelites and did not raise its head again. During Gideon's lifetime, the land enjoyed peace forty years.

(JUDGES 8:27–28)

STEP TEN

Why do the greatest failures seem to come after the greatest victories?

And why do God's leaders seem to go to such lengths to show how human they are?

We want our champions to stay on pedestals. We don't want them to step down or stumble, to become mere mortals again. However, the Bible shows us heroes who are real people, blemishes and all.

Real people fall. Worse, sometimes the greatest failures come after the biggest victories.

Adam and Eve, after God placed them in the most perfect paradise, celebrated by listening to the serpent, who ended up causing history's greatest swindle.

King David, at the height of his power, lusted after Bathsheba, failed miserably, and nearly destroyed his kingdom and family trying to cover up his sins.

So when Gideon blew it—and he did—he was in good company.

■ Gideon's Mistake

Gideon's compromise was not that he gained a lot of wealth. Money is just money, usable in any direction.

He clearly deserved a very high income. Would you agree with that? If we were all slaves today in America, suffering under the harsh rule of another nation and its dictator, wouldn't we give nearly everything we had to a champion who stood up, raised an army, and set us free?

The issue was not the money. Nowhere in Scripture will you hear, "And there was an ungodly amount of money made." We use terms like that today. We say, "He is filthy rich," or, "It's disgusting how much that person makes." But nowhere in Scripture is that phrase found. The truth is that there is no such thing as an "ungodly" amount of money, or being "filthy rich," or having a "sickening amount of money."

What there is, though, is a sickening use of money. There is a sickening way to handle wealth whether a person earns $30,000 a year or $30,000 a month or $30,000 an hour. It doesn't really matter. The issue is how you handle your money. What do you do with it?

I can show you people who have millions and millions of dollars and are very wise with that money in giving it to those in need and utilizing it far beyond themselves. I can also show you people who earn minimum wage and are extremely selfish and use every dime of their money for themselves.

Here is a quick measuring stick: If you want to know what you will do with wealth, take a look at what you are doing with your money right now. The biggest, most folly-filled trap most people fall into is in thinking, "Gee, if I were rich, everything would be great. I'd give half of everything I made to the church. I'd do this or that . . . "

But what are you doing now with what you have in your hands?

The best predictor of the future is your past. It doesn't have to stay that way. You can change. God has a better plan for you. But facts are facts until the vision gets bigger than the facts.

Money wasn't the problem with Gideon. The fact that he used part of his resources to build an idol in his hometown was a major-league problem.

■ The Ephod

Here is the "Cliffs Notes" version of how Gideon stumbled: He took a portion of the gold he received from his men, melted it down, and created a beautiful ephod—a priestly breastplate. In Israel, the high priest's breastplate represented spiritual authority. Ironically, Gideon had just refused to accept political power. Instead, he apparently decided to lay claim to spiritual authority. Or perhaps he was simply trying to set up a memorial of God's victory.

This idea probably looked good on paper. Gideon wanted to set up an outward symbol of God's blessing and protection. Perhaps this idea came from his previous feelings of inadequacy. Maybe Gideon felt incapable of being an instrument of God's guidance and direction for the nation of Israel and felt that he needed a visible symbol of it. Whatever the reason, the problem came when Gideon stopped listening to God's voice and started making up his own rules that ignored the ones given by the LORD:

> "Temptations discover what we are."
> — THOMAS À KEMPIS

> And God spoke all these words: "I am the LORD your God, who brought you out of Egypt, out of the land of slavery. You shall have no other gods before me. You shall not make for yourself an idol in the form of anything in heaven above or on the earth beneath or in the waters below. You shall not bow down to them or worship them; for I, the LORD your God, am a jealous God, punishing the children for the sin of the fathers to the third and fourth generation of those who hate me, but showing love to a thousand generations of those who love me and keep my commandments" (Exodus 20:1–6).

Gideon ignored that pesky first commandment, and what do you know? The result was excruciatingly predictable. The people turned the ephod into an idol by worshipping it instead of the *Lord* who had delivered them from Midian. Sound familiar?

Judges 2:27 says, "All Israel prostituted [King James Version: 'went to whoring'] themselves by worshipping it there, and it became a snare to Gideon and his family."

In the glow of a miraculous, historic, and total victory, Gideon messed up on a grand scale. However well-intentioned Gideon's ephod was, Israel was already prone to idolatry, and as time went on, it deserted God's altar and priesthood. Sadly, the nation was led into idol worship by one great man's false step. This false step became a snare to Gideon himself, to his family, and to his nation, all of whom were drawn into sin.

Instead of being remembered solely for what happened against the massive Midianite army and the historic military victory, Gideon's final chapter will always be a monument to the fact that past victories do not insure future successes.

■ Compromise

Unfortunately, I wish I could give you a better ending to the story. There were great results from Gideon's victory over the Midianites. The Bible tells us, "Thus Midian was subdued before the Israelites and did not raise its head again. During Gideon's lifetime, the land enjoyed peace forty years" (Judges 8:28). Peace for forty years is no small feat. Dealing effectively with the terrorists brought an end to intimidation and fear.

> "Holiness is not a series of dos and don'ts, but a conformity to God's character in the very depths of our being.
>
> This conformity is possible only as we are united with Christ."
>
> — JERRY BRIDGES

I wish the story of Gideon himself had ended well. It did not. When Gideon decided to make the ephod, he learned that, like it or not, leaders live in a fishbowl. No matter where you are or what you do, people are watching you. You may say, "It's none of their business how I live my life." Unfortunately, you don't live on an island alone, so it is their business. And whether you like it or not, how you live your life will influence people all around you.

So what was the problem with Gideon's ephod? Wasn't he just trying to commemorate God's great victory and remind the Israelites to give Him the glory? Maybe. But the ephod had exactly the opposite effect. It placed Gideon at the center of things. He shifted the focus away from God, away from the others on his team, and placed it squarely on himself. He took a blessing and turned it into a stumbling block. He would have done better to remember God's command to be holy—set apart—unto Him.

Leviticus 20:7 tells us, "Consecrate yourselves and be holy, because I am the LORD your God." However, holiness does not imply perfection. No one who has lived on earth—except Jesus—has been perfect. Nevertheless, holiness is an ideal for which to strive.

■ Holiness and Do-Overs

If you are hounded by your own internal guilt, or find yourself saying, "I messed up again," you are falling into a perfection trap. Remember, Jesus came to bring salvation, not condemnation:

> For God so loved the world that he gave his one and only Son, that whoever believes in him shall not perish but have eternal life. For God did not send his Son into the world to condemn the world, but to save the world through him. Whoever believes in him is not condemned, but whoever does not believe stands condemned already because he has not believed in the name of God's one and only Son. (John 3:16–18)

Holiness is pursuing the character of God. If you find yourself frustrated because you messed up again, you're in good company. Many Christians walk under a cloud of guilt because they fail to live up to the unrealistic expectation that they should be perfect.

This is not to say that we should justify our sin because of our humanity. Rather, we need to recognize that holiness is only made possible through the grace and power God offers through the Holy Spirit. That is why as I write these words, I'm almost in tears because I have been repeatedly given grace through Jesus Christ. As Paul said, "Thank God for Jesus!" Where would I be without His forgiveness?

"How little people know who think that holiness is dull. When one meets the real thing it is irresistible. If even 10 percent of the world's population had it, would not the whole world be converted—and happy—before the year's end?"

— C. S. LEWIS

My favorite classes in school were the ones with teachers who would give us a "redo." Maybe your teachers called them "do-overs," a term we also used on the playground.

Whatever you called them, it felt great to turn in a test, and after the teacher looked through the answers, she'd say, "Bil, come up here. Go do number 4, number 12, and the last one again."

Yes, it was a little embarrassing. Yes, I wish I could have completed all the answers perfectly the first time. Still, I loved the idea of do-overs. Instead of writing all over my paper and making it look as if someone had bled all over it, the teacher gave me the chance to learn how to do it right.

Not all of my teachers were that way. Some teachers seemed to delight in seeing how many students they could fail. It was almost as if they enjoyed all the red ink. Thank God for the teachers who loved to see you and me succeed.

God is like that. He wants to see you succeed. He is continually cheering you on.

God does not want to see us fail. The only red ink He uses is the blood of Christ on the cross: "For you know that it was not with perishable things such as silver or gold that you were redeemed from the empty way of life handed down to you from your forefathers, but with the precious blood of Christ, a lamb without blemish or defect" (1 Peter 1:18–19).

In fact, when you ask for God's forgiveness, the blood of Jesus Christ leaves your slate clean: "Though your sins are like scarlet, they shall be as white as snow; though they are red as crimson, they shall be like wool" (Isaiah 1:18).

God washes the slate so clean that "he does not treat us as our sins deserve or repay us according to our iniquities. For as high as the heavens are above the earth, so great is his love for those who fear him; as far as the east is from the west, so far has he removed our transgressions from us" (Psalm 103:10–12).

Maybe you keep failing in the same area again and again. Israel kept going back to the same sins over and over. Gideon's ill-conceived decision to build the golden ephod encouraged Israel's tendency toward idol worship.

> "The unexamined life is not worth living."
>
> — SOCRATES

You may have a recurring struggle that never seems to never go away. The good news is that God keeps giving you the paper back: "I know you failed last time, but you have a redo. And now I'm going to give you the chance to do it again, to do it right."

Isn't that great to know? Isn't it liberating to know that we serve a God of grace? He wants you to have a redo.

"But my marriage fell apart!" you say.

"Okay, here's a redo."

"But you have no idea what I've done in my past!" you say.

"Well, that's fine. Here's a redo, a do-over."

God gave me a do-over when we were still living in Dallas.

I was pastor of a small church, but nothing was going right. We only had about fifty people, but we weren't growing. I met with the leadership and tried to discuss our options, but ultimately we decided to just chalk it up as a failure and move on.

It would have been very easy to quit at that point, believing that God didn't want me to plant a church. After all, how do you go forward and do the same thing when you've already failed once? When I talked to my wife about going to Corpus Christi to start a church, her response was, "Like the one we're in now?" Thankfully, she believed in do-overs, too, and decided to support me in the move to plant a church again.

But I knew what God had called me to do. I had a strong sense of purpose. So I took the lessons I learned from that first church, and we formed Bay Area Fellowship. I did the same things that I'd done before, but the results were much different because having a clearer purpose shaped our actions into successful actions. Bay Area Fellowship is now one of the fastest growing churches in America.

Experiencing failure isn't necessarily an indication that you should give up. Sometimes the difference between someone who receives God's blessing and someone who doesn't is that the one who experiences God's blessing simply holds on longer than the other guy.

God wants you to know that you can be forgiven. He's saying, "Take a redo, a do-over, and this time do it right. It is okay. I love you. You are the reason that My Son endured the shame of the cross."

> "If adversity develops character, prosperity demands it."
>
> — J. D. EPPINGA

Bank on God's love and forgiveness, even when you fail. Bask in His love and forgiveness, even when you ask for a do-over.

Gideon blew it. He could have had a "do-over." All he needed to do was admit that he was wrong and destroy the golden ephod when he saw that the Israelites were worshipping it. For some reason, he chose not to.

There is much to learn from Gideon's life. Most of it is positive. Although the final lesson is negative, we can learn from it as well. Let Gideon's failure remind you to take advantage of God's do-overs. Along with your triumphs and successes, you will face obstacles, heartbreaks, tragedies, hindrances, and unavoidable problems. While most people tend to lose heart and surrender their dreams during life's horrible times, remember to press on, trusting in God's grace, forgiveness, and mercy.

When successful people fail, they think about what went wrong and what they can do differently the next time. Most of us can deal with success; however, it is what we do when we make a mistake that determines what we get out of life.

It does not matter how many mistakes you make or even how many times you fail on your road to success. What matters is that you learn from each failure and seek to improve your performance the next time around. You need to use what you learn to make better decisions about what you should do in the

> "Success is not the reverse of failure; it is the scorn of failure. Always dare to fail; never fail to dare."
>
> — STEPHEN S. WISE

future. Granted, you may be allowed fewer and fewer mistakes as you move up the success ladder, but you should never reach the point where you stop taking risks. The secret of long-term success is constantly seeking to correct your course.

Course Corrections

Make mistakes, but never allow yourself to wallow in failure. You must be creative, not reactive. Strength only comes through life's lessons and character building. When you face a challenge or a failure, say to yourself, "How can I make something good come out of this?"

Let's discuss nine course corrections that will help you overcome your failures or judgment errors.

DEFINE WHAT SUCCESS MEANS TO YOU
What is your mission?

A clear definition of what you want to accomplish in life will help you keep eventual success in perspective. Fantasyland is a cute place to visit at Disney World, but don't allow yourself to live in a dream world. Achieving success does not mean that you leave reality, failure, or problems behind. You need a clear idea of where you're going so that if and when you get off track, you'll know what changes you need to make. In a sense, knowing your mission—your purpose and goals—is like having a built-in GPS system. Be sure to take the time to define your goals and purpose.

LEARN FROM EXPERIENCE

If you don't learn from the past, you will be condemned to repeat it. When you fail, try to determine what caused that failure. Likewise, when you succeed, seek to understand what you did to produce positive results. As simplistic as it may seem, success is simply learning what does and does not work. There's no reason to beat yourself up emotionally when you make bad judgments. Resolve to learn all you can from your experiences.

SEEK COACHES TO MONITOR AND GUIDE YOU

In many instances, the best teacher is a mentor or coach who has the experience to help you make wise course corrections. Top sports professionals pay millions of dollars to coaches who carefully check to see if bad habits are creeping in to their technique. The best corporations in the world hire well-paid consultants to monitor each part of their operations and make recommendations for change. So why do we think it is difficult or unusual to have coaches and mentors in our lives to help us check vital signs and offer suggestions for success?

Incidentally, a coach doesn't have to be a highly paid consultant. A coach can simply be a wise friend, relative, pastor, counselor—someone whose opinion and knowledge you trust.

AIM HIGH

You have probably already noticed that successful people constantly talk and think and pursue dreams and goals. The reason should always be clear: Your goals make the difference between aimless wandering and effective action. It is hard to make good course corrections while you are drifting around haphazardly. Make sure your goals are clearly defined and reachable, but also challenging.

CONCENTRATE ON PRODUCTIVE EFFORT

I've found that most people spend the majority of their time aimlessly, merely doing busywork, as they wait for the "big" moments in life. If you want to be successful in making course corrections, you must focus on effective efforts all the time, even when the spotlight isn't focused on you. You must be actively pursuing your goals, not passively waiting for success to drop in your lap.

> "The successful man lengthens his stride when he discovers the signpost has deceived him; the failure looks for a place to sit down."
>
> — JOHN RUSKIN

KEEP MOVING

As part of monitoring your progress and making course corrections, it's important to keep setting new goals and dreams for yourself. Most people don't quit on life deliberately, but they give up their visions a piece at a time when they run into barriers or detours. Determine over and over what success means to you, and then do whatever is necessary to make the changes to achieve your dreams. You might need to revise and adjust your goals at times. Other times you may need to change them entirely. But never stop moving toward them.

LEARN TO UNDERSTAND THE DIFFERENCE BETWEEN STUMBLING BLOCKS AND STEPPING-STONES

You probably learned in seventh-grade science that "for every action, there is an equal and opposite reaction." If you do anything in life, anything at all, you will encounter opposition. You will fail. It is a fact. Still you cannot turn back every time you run into a wall or make a bad decision. It is not always easy to tell the difference between a stumbling block and a stepping-stone, especially when the obstacle seems to be ten feet tall. Nevertheless, resolve to climb over those stumbling blocks in your life and transform them into stepping-stones.

TREAT FAILURE AND SUCCESS THE SAME WAY

"The grand essentials to happiness in this life are something to do, something to love, and something to hope for."

— JOSEPH ADDISON

Every life has both victories and losses. Whatever happens, in any endeavor, you should always take time to stand back and examine why you succeeded or failed. Look at every step in life—whether forward or backward—as an opportunity to learn and grow. This attitude will prevent you from being blinded by your successes and defeated by your failures.

CONSTANTLY FOCUS ON TODAY AND TOMORROW RATHER THAN ON YOUR PAST

Be a champion goal-setter. You should make a regular practice of planning ahead, setting short-, mid-, and long-range goals. Along the way, spend time with people who love you for yourself, not for your successes. True friends—people who love you for the right reasons—will always point you toward the future. Learn to deal with failures, to ask forgiveness, and to make course corrections, but don't dwell on the past.

Looking Back–Looking Forward

In 1923, a group of the world's most successful financiers met at a Chicago hotel. Among those present were these nine men:

- the former president of the largest independent steel company in the world

- the nation's best-known wheat and commodity speculator

- the president of the New York Stock Exchange

- the secretary of the interior of President Harding's cabinet

- the president of the Bank of International Settlements

- the man known as the "Match King," who headed one of the world's prime monopolies

- the man who was one of the most successful stock speculators on Wall Street

- a past chairman of one of the country's largest utility companies

- the former president of the largest gas company in the United States.

Collectively, these tycoons controlled more wealth than existed in the United States treasury. For years newspapers and magazines had been printing their success stories. The youth of the nation had been challenged to follow the lofty examples of these nine men.

Twenty-five years later, the names remained etched in history, but time had changed everything:

- Charles Schwab, the president of Bethlehem Steel, lived on borrowed money the last five years of his life and died penniless.

- Arthur Cutten, the great wheat speculator, died abroad in poverty.

- Richard Whitney, former president of the New York Stock Exchange, served time in Sing Sing for grand larceny.

- Albert Fall, once a respected member of the president's cabinet, was pardoned from prison so he could die at home.

- Leon Fraser, president of the Bank of International Settlements, committed suicide.

- Ivar Krueger, the head of the world's greatest monopoly, the International Match Corporation, died tragically; whether he was murdered or committed suicide was never established.

- Jesse Livermore, called "the most wondrous of the boy wonders of Wall Street," died by suicide.

- Samuel Insull, once chairman of Commonwealth Edison Company and other utility corporations, was acquitted on embezzlement and mail-fraud charges. He died in Paris in modest surroundings.

- Howard Hopson, the president of the Associated Gas and Electric utility empire, served time in prison for mail-fraud charges and eventually died in a sanitarium.

All of these men had learned how to make money. All were considered to be top leaders. All were feted in the press. Nevertheless, their lives ended in failure. Their success was great, but for various reasons they failed to sustain that success. We don't have to judge these men or their standards. History has done that for us. Instead, we should learn from their mistakes, even as we learn from Gideon's bad judgment that led to Israel's return to idol worship.

I am reminded of a story I heard once about a successful man who was asked the secret of his accomplishments. His reply: "Good judgment."

"Where did you learn good judgment?" he was asked.

"From experience."

"And where did you gain your experience?"

"From bad judgment."

I have found that success and failure are almost always linked. I don't know anyone who has achieved much without suffering from bad judgment, defeats, and failures. In fact, a man or woman who has never been defeated is usually a person who has never tried, has never risked.

Don't flounder in your setbacks; be glad for them. Make course corrections. Keep moving. Don't stop. Problems and failures are great launching points. The difference between successful people and unsuccessful people is often their attitude toward mistakes and failure.

As I've mentioned, you may be allowed fewer and fewer mistakes as you move up the success ladder, but you can never reach the point where you stop taking risks.

Make mistakes, but never allow yourself to remain stuck in your misery. You must be creative, not reactive. Strength only comes through life lessons and character building. Say to yourself: "How can I make something good come out of this?"

Gideon failed; you will too.

The question is, what will you do with your failures and setbacks as you continue to learn how to live a life without limits?

The Apostle Paul knew about failure. He knew about wrong directions. He had studied the life of Gideon and knew what happens when you don't make course corrections. Under the inspiration of the Holy Spirit, Paul wrote the words that can help you keep going, no matter where you are in life: "But this one thing I do, forgetting those things which are behind, and reaching forth unto those things which are before, I press toward the mark for the prize of the high calling of God in Christ Jesus" (Philippians 3:13–14, KJV).

No matter what happens, anytime you mess up, ask God for forgiveness. Take a do-over. Press toward the mileposts ahead that tell you of the great rewards as you follow God's direction in your life.

When you fail, and you will, and when you feel like quitting, and you will, say to yourself, as you did when you started this book: "That's it! I'm going to continue to change. The next stage of my new life starts today—again. From this moment forward, with God's help, I will seek nothing less than God's best."

ACTION PLAN

?
■
At the beginning of this book, I asked you to look at your life and ask, "Where am I, and where do I want to *be* in five years?" Looking back over the book and what you have experienced as you read the pages, let's consider the question again. Where do you want to be five years from now?

Spend some time in prayer, asking God to help you think through your goals and to understand His will for you—what He wants you to do. Then, take out your notebook and write down your thoughts on the following questions:

1. What biggest inner challenges have you faced as you have gone through the book?

2. What are the greatest victories you have experienced while working through this book?

3. How have your goals changed as you have read this book?

4. How has your action plan changed as you have read this book?

5. Now that you've finished, what is your next step? What specifically will you do to move toward your goals today? Tomorrow? Next week?

Remember to keep moving toward your goals, trusting God's guidance as you go. Even if you have to adjust and change your goals and your action plan, keep pressing forward. That's the difference between dreaming of a better life and living it.

CONCLUSION

Now that you've come to the end of this book, one question remains: What will you do? Sadly, most people will probably put this book on the shelf and go on with their lives, completely unchanged by what they've read. They'll be like Dave, the newlywed I mentioned in the introduction.

Dave, you may remember, wanted to build a business in real estate, but he was stuck in neutral, not moving forward. He kept talking about how badly he wanted to be his own boss and have his own business, but he wasn't doing anything about it. I finally had to give Dave a nudge and tell him that he couldn't make another appointment with me until he had purchased his first rental property. That got Dave moving, and soon he was actively building a real estate portfolio and even started another business. All it took was a little nudge.

That's what I'd like to do with you too. Obviously, I can't nudge you like I did Dave. You're not in my office, and I can't tell you to do something before you make another appointment with me. But what I can do is encourage you to take action—be sure you've made a plan—before you go to sleep tonight.

In this book, you have learned practical principles for experiencing change and discovering God's best for your life. Each chapter has included action steps so that you can develop a plan. Maybe you did those exercises; maybe you didn't. If you worked through the exercises, you're already well on your way to changing your life. But if you didn't, what are you waiting for? Perhaps you wanted to read through the whole book and get an overview before you started working on the exercises. If so, it's time now to go back and start on them in earnest.

Remember that success is a process of day-by-day accomplishment. If you really want your life to change for the better, you have to take action. You have to *do* something . . . every day.

So what are you going to do?

Are you going to break your cycle of failure? Have you reached your pain threshold? Are you ready to go a different direction with your life? Are you ready to build a team? If you are, then when you finish reading the next few paragraphs, I want you to do several things.

First, take a piece of paper or an index card and write down one thing that you really want to change about your life. Maybe it's something that has come to mind as you've read through this book. Or perhaps it's a situation that made you pick up the book in the first place. Whatever you choose to start with, don't make your goal so big that it's overwhelming. But don't make it so easy that it's a slam dunk either. I want you to challenge yourself.

Second, write down specifically what you are going to do to begin the process of change. For example, maybe you want to spend less time watching television and more time reaching out to other people. Make your goal specific. Write down something like "For the next month, I'm going to watch no more than one hour of TV per day and I'm going to invest the extra time helping with the church homeless ministry.

Third, make sure that your goal is measurable and that you have a deadline. Remember that I told Dave he couldn't make another counseling appointment until he'd bought his first rental property? The measurable goal was buying the first rental property. The deadline: no more appointments with me until he'd reached the goal.

Fourth, find someone who will hold you to your goal. In other words, become accountable. Dave was accountable to me, his pastor. In your case it might be a spouse, a parent, a good friend, an employer or your pastor. Accountability is essential if you really want to accomplish the goals you set. You need someone who will cheer you on when you're getting discouraged and thinking about quitting. And you need someone who will rejoice with you when you make that goal.

Finally, remember to seek God's help and His will in this process. Gideon became a mighty warrior because God was with him. He recognized God's call on his life. Then he took the risk and laid everything on the line. God rewarded his faith.

God will reward your faith, too, as you seek His will in your life. Press on toward God's best—every day.

THE DARE TO CHANGE CHALLENGE

WHAT'S YOUR PLAN?

Making changes in your life is so important, so much a part of what God wants for you, that I'm going to make one more suggestion. Except this time it's more than a suggestion; it's a dare to change!

If you've read carefully through this book and taken the ten steps to heart, and if you've worked through the simple exercises, then I want to know your plan. I dare you to make it all the more real by typing it up or putting pen to paper and sending it to me. Keep it as simple or as lengthy as you want. I would love to hear about your plan to experience change and discover more of God's best.

I not only want to know your plan, but as time goes on, I also want to know what you do to realize it. I want to hear about any successes and changes you experience in the coming weeks or months. Perhaps you'll accomplish something simple yet real and tangible, or perhaps your achievement will be huge and remarkable. Perhaps you'll make a life-changing decision to follow Christ and a whole new world will open up for you. I want to hear about it all!

Please send in your plan and your stories of success, including your name, address, e-mail address and phone number to:

Bil Cornelius Ministries
7451 Bay Area Drive
Corpus Christi, Texas 78415

ACKNOWLEDGMENTS

The book you hold in your hands is proof-positive of what can be accomplished when we listen for God's call, break out of boundaries, develop a new attitude, create a plan and put together a team to make it all happen.

In my case, I'm in awe and wonder of God for allowing me the privilege to write this book. Having been a part of the writing process, I must tell you that you never write a book alone.

I'm completely and totally overwhelmed with gratitude for my wife, Jessica; for her wise counsel and immense patience. I'd like to thank my family: Mason, Cole and Sophie for letting their dad "have just a few more minutes on this book." For my mom and dad, Ann and Bill Cornelius, Pam and Daniel Korus, Tom and Claire Lander (you raised an amazing daughter!), and David and Meredith Alexander. A special thanks for your constant support and encouragement to Jay and Sofia Lyons and Will and Leslie Lewis.

My deep gratitude goes to my mentors, Ed Young, Rick Warren and Craig Groeschel, whose guidance gave me the room and encouragement to discover so much of God's plan for my life. I am also indebted to Craig not only for the mentoring but also for the amazing foreword. I'm blessed with an incredible team here at Bay Area Fellowship, including Paul Schulz, Brian Fiscus, John Atkinson, Scott

Downey, Don Fine (you rock!), Aaron Guevara (world's greatest assistant!), Monica Carrion (great photos!), Mark Marquez, Joe MacArthur, Trish Frazier (thanks for all the "publicity"), and too many to mention each by name. I also would like to thank the church that has changed my life, Bay Area Fellowship: I am blessed to get to be your pastor.

Thanks to Darryl Hicks and James Pence for helping this book take form. I'm thankful for my agent, Rachelle Gardner, for helping me extend this ministry through the world of publishing, as well as for the team at Guideposts Books, including Editor-in-Chief Linda Cunningham, my editor David Morris (you make my thoughts actually make sense), marketer extraordinaire Carl Raymond (your energy knows no limits), sales directors Marty Flanagan and Debbie Felt (thanks for believing in this), and so many others. Thank you, A. Larry Ross and the whole team at ALR Communications, for stirring things up in the media for this book.

May all of our efforts help each of us to go big, dare to change and discover the extraordinary life God has in store.

Regardless of how this book gig turns out, I'd like to thank my Lord and Savior Jesus Christ, who saved me by grace alone. Trust me on this one . . . grace . . . alone.